P9-CSW-801

# WALKS IN HEMINGWAY'S PARIS

# WALKS IN HEMINGWAY'S PARIS
## A Guide to Paris for the Literary Traveler

Noël Riley Fitch

*St Martin's Griffin* ☙ *New York*

WALKS IN HEMINGWAY'S PARIS. Copyright © 1989 by Noel Riley Fitch. All rights reserved. Printed in the United States of America. No part of this book may be used or reproduced in any manner whatsoever without writen permission except in the case of brief quotations embodied in critical articels or reviews. For inforamation, address St. Martin's Press, 175 Fifth Avenue, New York, NY 10010.

Library of Congress Cataloging-in-Publication Data
Fitch, Noel Riley.
    Walks in Hemingway's Paris: a guide to Paris for the literary traveler/
Noel Riley.
    p.    cm.
    ISBN 0-312-07113-2
    1. Hemingway, Ernest, 1899-1961—Homes and haunts—France—
Paris.  2. Literaty landmarks—France—Paris—Guidebooks.  3.
Walking—France—Paris—Guidebooks.  4. Authors, American—20th
century—Biography.  5. Americans—France—Paris—History—20th
century.  6. Paris (France)—Description—1975—Guidebooks.  I. Title.
PS3515.E3725934    1990
813'.52—dc20
[B]                                                       90-8609
                                                             CIP


First published in Great Britain by the Thorson Publishing Group


10 9 8 7 6

**To Bertie**
with whom life is *une fête*

# CONTENTS

# WALKS IN HEMINGWAY'S PARIS

# ACKNOWLEDGEMENTS

To the National Endowment for the Humanities, I am indebted for two travel grants. To my summer students at the American University of Paris, who walked the streets of Paris with these maps, I am grateful for valuable suggestions. My special gratitude to Gailyn Robin Fitch, my daughter and friend, who set this manuscript in type and offered moral support.

I also wish to thank Princeton University Library (Sylvia Beach Papers, F. Scott Fitzgerald Papers, Charles Scribner Papers); Newberry Library, Chicago (Malcolm Cowley Correspondence); Kennedy Library, Boston (Ernest Hemingway Papers); Beinecke Rare Books and Manuscript Room, Yale (Bryher Papers, Stein Papers); and the Harry Ranson Humanities Research Center of the University of Texas, Austin.

Of the many participants who told me their stories of Paris over the last 18 years, I especially thank the following: Kay Boyle, André Chamson, Morrill Cody, the late Caresse Crosby, the late Malcolm Cowley, Leon Edel, the late Janet Flanner, the late Marcelle Fournier, the late Florence Gilliam, the late Archibald MacLeish, the late Hadley Hemingway Mowrer, George Seldes, the late Solita Solano, the late Allen Tate, and the late Thornton Wilder.

I also owe a great debt to those who have shared their more recent knowledge of Paris with me: Keeler and Colette Faus, Warren and Jean Trabant, and Phil and Mary Hyman, all long-time residents of Paris; Odile Hellier of the Village Voice bookshop in Paris; and Albert Sonnenfeld, with whom I share the feast of Paris.

I am grateful to the several scholars and biographers who were helpful in clarifying facts and reading portions of this manuscript: Matthew J. Bruccoli, Robert Gajdusek, James Hinkle, Ernest Kroll, and Michael Reynolds. During the final stages of my work, Professor Reynolds generously shared with me his manuscript of the second volume of his biography of Hemingway, *Hemingway: The Paris Years*.

For permission to quote material here, I am indebted to Criterion Books, publisher of Harold Loeb's *The Way It Was* (1959); Doubleday and Company for quotations from André Le Vot's *F. Scott Fitzgerald: A Biography* (1983) and Robert McAlmon and Kay Boyle's *Being Geniuses Together* (1968); Harcourt Brace, publisher of Sylvia Beach's *Shakespeare and*

*Company* (1959); Houghton Mifflin, publisher of Archibald MacLeish's 'His Mirror Was Danger' in *New and Collected Poems, 1917-1982* (1985), MacLeish's *A Continuing Journey* (1968), and Paul Scott Mowrer's *The House of Europe* (1945); Liveright for quotations from Gertrude Stein's *Paris France* (1970) and E.E. Cummings's *Is 5* (1926); New Directions, publisher of Ezra Pound's 'In the Station of the Metro' from *Personae* (1926, 1990); New American Library, publisher of Françoise Gilot and Charlton Lake's *Life With Picasso* (1965); Curtis Brown, publisher of William Faulkner's *Sanctuary* (1958); Charles Scribner's Sons, publisher of books by F. Scott Fitzgerald: *Tender is the Night* (1933, 1962), *The Stories of F. Scott Fitzgerald*, edited by Malcolm Cowley (1951, 1979), *The Great Gatsby* (1925, 1953), *The Letters of F. Scott Fitzgerald*, edited by Andrew Turnbull (1963 Frances Scott Fitzgerald); The Ernest Hemingway Foundation and Charles Scribner's Sons, publisher of works by Ernest Hemingway: *By-Line: Ernest Hemingway*, edited by William White (1968), *Green Hills of Africa* (1936, 1963), *The Nick Adams Stories* (1972), *Islands in the Stream* (1970), *A Moveable Feast* (1964), *Selected Letters*, edited by Carlos Baker (1981), and *The Sun Also Rises* (1926, 1954); Simon & Schuster, publisher of William Shirer's *20th Century Journey; 1904-1930* (1976); Charles Scribner's Sons, publishers of Thomas Wolfe's *Of Time and the River* (1935, 1971); Viking Press, publisher of Malcolm Cowley's *Second Flowering* (1973).

For permission to reproduce photographs not my own, I wish to thank Robert E. Gajdusek, Gisèle Freund, Princeton University, and Roger-Viollet of Paris.

# AN INTRODUCTION TO PARIS

The writer needs a sense of place, a place to put down roots even if those roots must be torn out as he starts on his journey to independence. This place of origin nourishes his soul: he knows its people, their proverbs and dialects; he knows their aspirations and their failures. Through his sense of place the writer comes to know himself. The voyage, therefore, begins at home, for that home is the writer's reality, no matter how far he may wander in forging his art.

Most artists leave the place of their origin — the place that formed their youth and their sense of reality. They leave as a result of maturation, family moves, education, or career. Those artists whose place is provincial may feel their alienation from that culture. Some of these artists from the provinces flee in anger the cultural insularity or the ugliness of home. Others seek what they do not have in their place of origin. They may seek acceptance for their art and a community with other artists. In the first three decades of this century, an unprecedented number of artists from various countries of the world sought this community of artists in Paris.

The artists of the early twentieth century did not invent deracination, but they did make it a vogue. They discovered that Paris helped them to solve their problem of inner exile, it fostered their maturity. Like artists before and since, they discovered that distance from home fuels interest in homeland and a keen and objective perspective on place. Hemingway wrote his story of Nick fishing in the Big Two-Hearted River in a café in Montparnasse. James Joyce wrote about Dublin in Zurich, Trieste, and Paris. Picasso painted *Guernica* just a block from the Seine. And Chagall painted the folklore and farm animals of his native Russia in a cramped hovel in the 15th arrondissement of Paris. They lived in a foreign country yet recreated the culture of their own land.

That Paris has been the second home for artists for centuries is no accident. The City of Light has represented the best in Western culture. 'It was a place where the very air was impregnated with the energies of art', wrote Thomas Wolfe. One sees this in the beauty of the architecture of the grand boulevards and monuments as well as in the names of its streets, for Paris honours its artists and philosophers. Paris has always accepted and nourished genius. Thus, it promises a haven to the fleeing or seeking artist. It is the ancient city of the exiled and the centre of Western art.

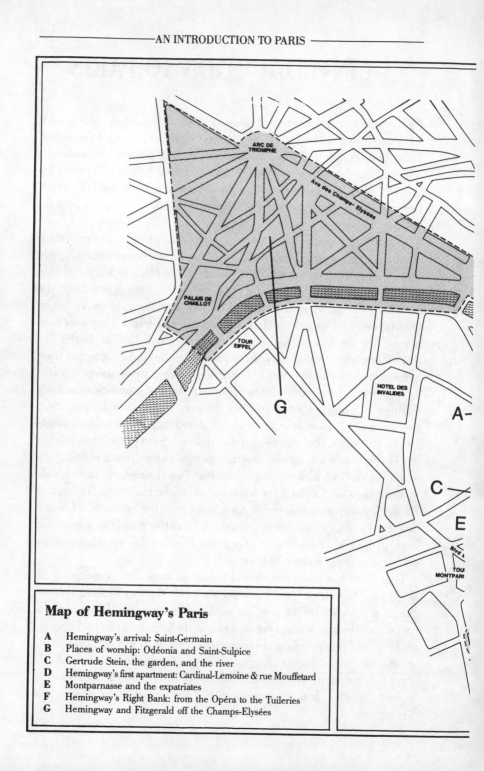

## Map of Hemingway's Paris

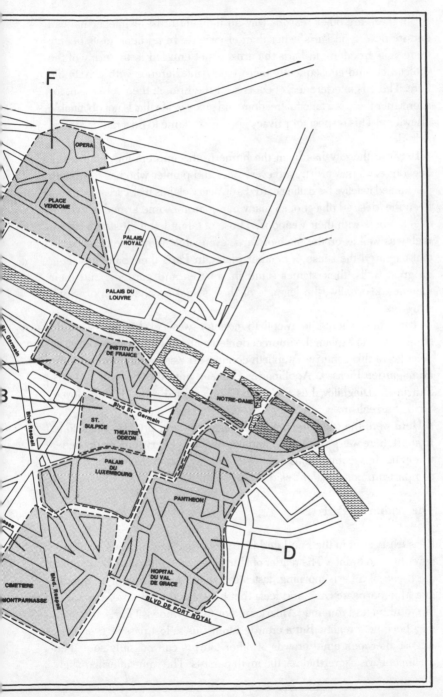

But there are other reasons why an indigent artist or intellectual can endure poverty in Paris better than elsewhere. In addition to its beauty there is its freedom; in Paris the artist is not enlisted in the army of the proletariat, and consequently there is less interference with private life here. There is interference, of course, for the French themselves, but for a foreigner there is a fanciful freedom and grace of life that is not obtainable elsewhere. This respect for privacy appears to some to be a rather amoral attitude.

Because the city has been the home of the masters for centuries, it beckons each new artist. And every poet and painter who has lived here has wanted to leave his calling card. Paul Valéry claims that Paris has always been the 'desired object of so many conquerors, some armed with their talent, others with their weapons'. Those of talent left their stamp on the reality as well as on the myth of Paris, even while they were creating art that captured the sense of another place. In Paris their paintings hang on great walls, their statues stand in squares and gardens, and their memoirs keep alive the legends of their social escapades and artistic struggles.

'Paris was where the twentieth century was', exclaimed Gertrude Stein — as if to explain the unprecedented gathering of artists in the early decades of this century. Twentieth-century art was being created by the avant-garde: Picasso, Apollinaire, Cubism and the School of Paris, Stravinsky, Diaghilev, Les Six, Nadia Boulanger, Proust, Pound, Joyce, Stein, Surrealism.

Here were the teachers, the little magazines and presses, the salons. In short, here was an audience, and acceptance. 'Every man works better when he has companions . . . yielding the stimulus of suggestion, comparison, consultation', said Henry James.

**The patina of Paris**

Paris exists even in the mind and hearts of artists and readers who have never been to France. The reader of Hemingway's *A Moveable Feast* smells the bread of a Paris morning, tastes the sharp, cool drink of an aperitif in a Montparnasse café, and feels that he walks the streets of Paris with the youthful and romantic American. For those who visit Paris, the myth may become a reality. But a crowded tour bus, a lost passport, or a hot August afternoon amid crowds of other tourists can possibly sour their dream of Paris. Nevertheless, the myth persists. The same afternoon light strikes the same building; the Seine still flows by the mighty Notre Dame Cathedral and by the trees at the tip of Ile de la Cité; and the cafés of Hemingway and Picasso continue to serve the same drinks (except for poisonous absinthe).

Paris is always old and always seeking the new. Past generations of artists draw us here as they themselves were drawn by earlier artists. Each generation makes Paris its own — each builds its memories and houses on top of the old. Paris beckons today's seeker to walk the old paths but to find his own Paris. 'There is never any ending to Paris', writes Hemingway, 'and the memory of each person who has lived in it differs from that of any other.' Each artist who has lived here has felt its influence and has enriched this century of creativity. This Paris glows with what Anaïs Nin calls 'a patina of shared lives'.

## Riverrun

Looping through the landscape of Paris is the river god that gave it birth and early protection from invaders. Today the spirits of the arts reside along the banks of the river — in the Louvre, the Picasso Museum, the Grand Palais, and the Petit Palais on its right, and the Musée d'Orsay, art schools, and galleries on its left. The spirits of the intellect look down on the river from the hill of the Sorbonne and Panthéon on the Left Bank. In the centre of the river arises a monument to the religious spirit, the Cathedral of Notre Dame.

Paris is one of the few great cities that has integrated the river into its life and art. For cities such as London and Berlin, the rivers are half gutter and divide the city. Though the Seine does divide a left of intellectual life and a right of commerce, it in fact unites the city as its natural centre. The Seine is used as the Venetians use the Piazza San Marco. It has drawn the best to its quays: one of the world's great palaces (Louvre), a great cathedral (Notre Dame), centres of administration (Chambre des Députés, Préfecture de Police, Palais de Justice), gardens (Tuileries), and the Eiffel Tower. No single one of these dominates the river, which is central. Add two island gems, beautiful bridges, bookstalls, trees, and fishermen, and it is little wonder that Baudelaire, Rilke, Wagner, and Joyce chose to live near its banks.

Up until the eighteenth century, more of the city traffic was by water than by road. Now cars and motor bikes, the latter noisier and seemingly more life-threatening, race along both river banks and cut across the

Ile de la Cité near its prow, Pont-Neuf. Floating more quietly behind the Cité is the narrower Ile Saint-Louis. The stone *quais* of the Seine are best seen from a boat. Although the 60-ton *bateaux-mouches* were abolished in 1934, one can take an excursion ride on a light tourist boat through the centre of town. If one is walking along the river at night, the spotlights from these boats illuminate the grand façades along the banks, enchanting the night and the city.

## Through circular districts

Paris is divided into 20 districts or 'arrondissements' (e), numbered chronologically in three concentric circles radiating from the Ile de la Cité, the heart of the city. For example, on the Left Bank along the Seine lie the 5e (including the Latin Quarter and the Sorbonne), the 6e (Saint-Germain-des-Prés and Luxembourg), and the 7e (Tour Eiffel, Invalides, and UNESCO). With the rational order of the French, each district has a city hall and a police station.

In turn each of these arrondissements is divided into four quarters for postal and other neighbourhood services. Because every map, guide book, dining guide, and street address refers to arrondissement, and because the Parisians themselves identify with the character of their own arrondissement or quarter, the visitor to Paris soon learns to use and benefit from the organization of the Parisian landscape.

In central Paris, especially in the first ten arrondissements, one can observe immediately why this is a grand city on a very human scale. The architecture is harmonious and no building is over five or six floors high. With the exception of the ugly Montparnasse Tower, no tall buildings block the sky of inner Paris, and the morning and afternoon light everywhere strikes the grey–white buildings of Paris. Also, the inner city is residential — people live everywhere and buy their bread and produce in their own street or neighbourhood.

Each stone has a history, yet amid these old structures a people live in the present, welcoming innovative change in design, fashion, and music. Sacré Coeur, the Eiffel Tower, Notre Dame, and the spires of the churches are the certainties; around them contemporary life flourishes: young people skate or break-dance, and restaurants flourish, die, and reopen under new management. The telephone system introduces a computerized telephone book — though its telephone lines run through seventeenth-century walls. These changes keep Paris the same.

Those who stay long in Paris become as concerned — some have said obsessed — with good food as are the French. They also develop a loyalty to one particular quarter of the city. Hemingway loved the Place de la Contrescarpe, with its narrow steep streets and the winos sleeping under the trees of the square. Joyce preferred the quiet of the Eiffel Tower quarter and liked to dine in expensive restaurants. Pablo Picasso and Natalie Barney, the American who ran the most famous salon, preferred the Saint-Germain-des-Prés quarter. Ford Madox Ford, the distinguished English novelist and friend of Hemingway and Joyce, was as decisive as the other visitors. Ford chose the Notre-Dame des Champs quarter:

I *detest* the Quartier de l'Etoile — that region not so much of the idle rich as of the too industrious rich — the bankers. I dislike all the boulevards built by Haussmann and his imitators. On the other hand I really love the real Quartier Latin, the Faubourg St. Germain, the streets between the Sorbonne and the Pantheon. I can even support the Boulevard Montparnasse though my Paris ends with the parallel rue Notre Dame des Champs. It is a grey, very quiet quarter with the gardens of the Luxembourg like a great green jewel on its breast.

The favourite quarter of this writer is the old quarter between the Place Saint-Germain-des-Prés, the Seine and the Boul' Mich'. This quarter is rich in literary and art history, yet its narrow, curving streets teem with students and artists. I enjoy seeing film revivals in the little theatres here. And on my way back to my place in the rue de Sèvres, I enjoy stopping in the Place Furstenberg in anticipation of hearing some late-afternoon or evening music. For me Paris is also a freshly baked *ficelle*, lovers kissing in the street, the *menu dégustation* in a good restaurant, an early spring evening on the terrace of the Deux Magots, and a late-night walk home along the river. It is a style of living that focuses on pleasure and beauty.

**The early years of this century**

For the foreign artists in the first decades of this century, Paris was charged with the aura of time and history. Lambert Strether (in Henry James's *The Ambassadors*), standing in Gloriana's garden, senses this same charged atmosphere, 'the sense of names in the air, of ghosts at the windows, of signs and tokens, a whole range of expression, all about him, too thick for prompt discrimination'. So too it was for the foreign artists in the decades after James. They arrived by train, bursting with excitement and intoxicated by their proximity to cathedrals, squares, and parks saturated for centuries with the imagination of artists and kings. Riding in the horse-drawn street-car through the spacious Right Bank boulevards, past the harmonious buildings, the foreign artist undoubtedly noted these signs and tokens of an atmosphere 'too thick for prompt discrimination'. This visitor passed the gardens of the Louvre, the green *quais* of the Seine, the pavement *pissoirs*.

In the narrow, cobblestone streets of the Left Bank, he probably heard the horses' hooves echo against the buildings which crowd each narrow sidewalk. In this neighbourhood of small shops, nothing seems standardized or machine-made. The small *pension* or resident hotel was then presided over by a little woman in black dress. The marble fireplace, gilt clock, antimacassars, garish wallpaper, and red plush chairs may have charmed him. The toilet facility off the stairway on each floor either charmed or frustrated each visitor, who squatted on a footrest raised on either side of the hole in the floor, reached for a piece of newspaper stuck on a nail on the wall, and pulled the chain above. Each visit to the tiny water-closet was a test for weak thigh muscles. But few of these foreign artists stopped to unpack before rushing for their first aperitif at the Dôme or Rotonde and a late evening of listening and gawking in wonder in Montparnasse.

The morning only intensified the charged atmosphere: the taste of rich, steamy *café au lait* and flaky bottomed croissant; the sound of wagon loads of hay, vegetables and fruits, with dew still on the berries; the cry of street vendors, each with a refrain to announce the sharpening of knives, the shining of shoes, or the selling of vegetables or flowers. The visitor bought a guidebook at a colourful kiosk, looked bashfully through the window of Shakespeare and Company at No. 12 rue de l'Odeón, strolled down the Boulevard Saint-Michel to the bookstalls along the Seine. The gothic façade of Notre Dame, perhaps the chief sign of time and history in Paris, drew the visitor into its dark interior. There the sunlight streamed in through thirteenth-century stained glass.

After a day of pressing the cobblestones and absorbing the ghosts of history, he walked home through the rue de l'Odéon, past the Odéon theatre and the Senate building to the Luxembourg Gardens, where he heard the merry-go-round and watched the children in their immaculate uniforms sailing coloured boats in the pond after school.

Tomorrow admission is free at the Louvre and the visitor can see older stones and monuments from Egypt, Persia, Greece, and Rome. With guidebook in hand, he will walk though numerous corridors seeking *Winged Victory, Venus de Milo,* and *Mona Lisa.* There will be a 25-cent top balcony seat at the Opéra, a 50-cent borrowers' subscription at Shakespeare and Company, a free lecture at the Collège de France or the Sorbonne — where he can hear Bergson or Santayana. And within days he may find a cheap studio to share with another artist, or a job as a clerk at his consulate or a copyreader at a foreign newspaper. Paris will soon begin to feel like home.

**On finding this past today**

The Paris that the foreign artist found is largely still here to be found: buildings where they lived, cafés where they drank. There are, of course, several jarring visual changes if one returns to Paris. Though only the Montparnasse Tower breaks the harmony of the inner city, the distant horizon is now dotted with high-rise apartment buildings. And the great food market (Les Halles), the belly of Paris, is gone; in its place is an enormous hole filled with hundreds of crowded shops and modern architecture. Nearby is the Centre Georges Pompidou, which looks like a steamship or a factory turned inside out, supported by red, blue, and green pipes. A huge glass pyramid now rises from the inner courtyard of the Louvre. The wine market on the Left Bank has been replaced by a branch of the university that looks like a concrete prison. Several blocks behind the Montparnasse Tower have been levelled, and many cobblestoned streets paved. Yet the visitor may never notice these minor changes; indeed, he may love the new Halles. For compared to other Western cities, Paris is remarkably constant, protecting its beauty.

The daily life has changed little, though the pace has quickened and the number of visitors increased. Gone are the blue pneumatics (express letters), made unnecessary by the number of telephones. A regular letter mailed in the morning is still delivered by the next day. Bread is baked three not fives times a day. And the smelly *pissoirs* have been replaced by fewer, mechanized, private pay toilets. Many hallway toilets have been modernized or boarded up for private facilities. Buses have replaced horses and street-cars, and the métro runs on quiet rubber tyres. Wine bottles no longer take a deposit, but are collected in large green containers in the streets. But the water still flows along the gutters in early morning, sweeping the butts of Gitanes and Gauloises into the sewers.

Especially in the arts, change seems to hold and renew the essence of Paris. Impressionist paintings are no longer in the small galleries of the Palais du Luxembourg but in their new, spectacular home in the Musée d'Orsay. The Closerie des Lilas, where artists have gathered for nearly a century, no longer has any lilac bushes. But writers continue to write in a café in the early morning, and new literary magazines are born in the expatriate community. The bookshops and galleries are still crowded. The shops are still small, intimate, and stylishly displayed.

Underneath the superficial changes, the stones and the habits remain. The visitor can find the Paris of the early decades of this century and make his own correspondence with the landscape.

## Why Hemingway?

Ernest Hemingway is probably the most famous American expatriate to serve his literary apprenticeship in Paris. Here he honed his style and created his life as a struggling artist; here his fame had its genesis. He knew the streets of the city and wrote about his favourite places in short stories, novels, and a memoir.

Naturally, a focus on the Paris of one charismatic figure inevitably includes numerous artists. Active and social, Hemingway drew others into his orbit. Thus, his Paris includes the activities and writings of John Dos Passos, F. Scott Fitzgerald, E. E. Cummings, Janet Flanner, Gertrude Stein, and dozens of other Americans. He also had important exchanges with several English and French writers, and these artists are included.

A focus on the Americans in Paris risks reinforcing the misconception that the artistic renaissance of foreign artists in Paris during the first four decades of this century was an American phenomenon. On the contrary, artists from dozens of countries made the city their temporary or permanent home. There were more than twice as many British as Americans in Paris. They came for similar reasons: the cheap franc, the city's hospitality to art and artists, the presence of leaders of the avant-garde and, thus, both audience and publication outlets for experimental work. Other reasons for expatriation or exile ( the difference lay in the artist's attitude) differ from country to country, person to person. Like many Americans, Hemingway needed a supportive apprenticeship away from an unfriendly small town; Ford Madox Ford and many English wished to join the avant-garde activities; James Joyce fled Catholic Ireland; Marc Chagall and many other Eastern European artists fled anti-Semitism.

Hemingway's Paris differs from the Paris of James Joyce, or the Paris of Pablo Picasso and Marc Chagall, or the Paris of Henry Miller. The middle-aged Joyce, for example, found Paris a quiet place to work; his publishers and financial backers supported him in his longest single place of exile from Ireland. Joyce, Picasso, Miller, as well as Stein and other women, deserve their own volumes.

Though Hemingway may be the best-known American expatriate in Paris between the wars, it was the women who arrived first and stayed longer. Edith Wharton (1905), Natalie Barney (1902), Gertrude Stein (1903), and Sylvia Beach (1917) were here before Hemingway's arrival (1921). Stein, Beach, and the women who came during the 1920s — Janet Flanner, Djuna Barnes, Margaret Anderson and Nancy Cunard — played important roles in Hemingway's apprenticeship.

Rather than being a general guidebook to Paris streets, therefore, this book focuses on a single artist in order better to recreate the Paris of the particular period and to convey the particular effect that Parisian places had on one writer's life and work. The environment in which Hemingway lived and wrote certainly influenced his art. For example, in *A Moveable Feast* he describes his search on a cold rainy day for a warm clean café in which to write. After ordering a *café au lait* he pulled a pencil and notebook from his pocket and wrote. 'I was writing about up in Michigan', he remembers, 'and since it was a wild, cold, blowing day it was that sort of day in the story'. But the city did more than colour his mood or direct his selection of detail or subject. In many instances, the city became his subject matter. Here is the cityscape of Hemingway's fiction as well as a precise identification of the places where he rested, played, worked, and drank.

**On using this guide**

This book is written for the curious novice who wishes a more personal, intimate introduction to Paris — a knowledge beyond the Eiffel Tower and Notre Dame. It is also written for the seasoned traveller and expert who wishes to connect his reading and appreciation of the arts to particular buildings and to personal experience. Each reader can explore his own interest.

Walks on the **Left Bank (A–E)** and the two on the **Right Bank (F, G)** lead into each other. If you take them separately, however, there are clear directions from the closest métro (subway) to each walk. Needless to say, walking shoes and a bus/métro pass (a *carnet* of 10 tickets costs less than 30 francs) will add to the comfort and convenience of an excursion. A *Plan de Paris par arrondissement* is also a wise investment. In making your plans, remember that on Sunday the streets are less crowded, but more doors are closed, especially those to private residences.

It will be helpful to know that street numbers are assigned in relation to the river. Those streets that are roughly parallel to the Seine are numbered from east to west, as flows the river. Those streets that are approximately perpendicular to the river are numbered from the river. The odd numbers are on the left as you walk 'up' the street and do not always correspond closely to the even numbers opposite them (for example, 182 may face 121). I have used 'up' and 'down' to refer to the higher and lower numbers, not to the elevation of the street.

The maps have been organized for *flânerie*, which means wandering aimlessly with the intent of missing nothing. The journey itself is the goal. Stop for the street music, and allow time for coffee and lunch. A final word from the English novelist Lawrence Durrell, who warns against too much factual detail in travelling. One should, he declares, 'travel with the eyes of the spirit wide open'. The visitor should sit quietly and observe and smell and listen for the 'spirit of the place', which Durrell says is the 'most important determinant' in culture. Tune in, without reverence, idly, he adds, 'but with real inward attention'.

# 1

# HEMINGWAY'S PARIS

There is never any ending to Paris and the memory of each person
who has lived in it differs from that of any other. We always returned
to it no matter who we were or how it was changed or with what
difficulties, or ease, it could be reached. Paris was always worth it
and you received return for whatever you brought to it. But this is
how Paris was in the early days when we were very poor and very
happy.

Ernest Hemingway

Paris is 'the city I love best in all the world', declared Ernest Hemingway.
Though later he may have preferred life in other Latin countries, Paris
was the scene of his apprenticeship, of the best years of his life. It was
the 'moveable feast' he would evoke in his only memoir — his veritable
anthem to the city — *A Moveable Feast* (1959).

Few writers have been more place-conscious than Hemingway, as
he himself later acknowledged in his *Paris Review* interview with
George Plimpton, and in *A Moveable Feast*. In both accounts his emphasis
was on the necessity of writing in places that were conducive to clear
thinking and intense feeling. The sense of place and the sense of fact
were vitally linked to his art. He would implant each novel in its own
geography — noting even what time it was on each page. For the artist
as a young man, the place was Paris. He taught himself to write in this
city. His sense of fact drew him to its streets — he walked every street
and square and bridge of the central city. The young artist became
inexorably linked to this place.

Hemingway completed his education away from Oak Park, Illinois, where
he was born in 1899. He was the son of pious, middle-class parents
(a music teacher and a doctor) and his early acquaintances in Paris thought
the Midwesterner was a shy man, serious about his work. He had been
a cub reporter for the *Kansas City Star* after his graduation from Oak Park
High School. Then he was wounded in 1918 in Italy, where he was driving
an ambulance for the Red Cross. Afterwards he took a job as a reporter

for the *Toronto Star*. Because he wanted to be a writer, and at the suggestion of Sherwood Anderson, he moved to Paris, three years after the Armistice.

Although Hemingway had already been in Paris once for about 24 hours in June 1918 (on his way to Milan), his first true introduction to the city was in December of 1921. He arrived with his bride, Hadley Richardson, to write freelance articles for the *Toronto Star*. They had a patrimony belonging to Hadley that essentially supported them. They had letters of introduction from Sherwood Anderson, but they knew no one in the city. Hadley, who had studied French for eight years, served as translator until her husband learned street French, which he did quickly. Hemingway's first stop was the Hôtel Jacob et d'Angleterre in the Saint-Germain-des-Prés area — a first stop for many visiting artists. Soon he and Hadley were living off the Place de la Contrescarpe on Mont Sainte-Geneviève. He briefly rented a room around the corner on rue Descartes and worked there on his short stories with dedication and determination. Though he loved this old, poor section of Paris, it was a distance from most of his new friends — those who were leaders in the literary world.

Paris was a magnet for important people — people who would be significant to Hemingway's development: Gertrude Stein had arrived in 1902, Sylvia Beach in 1917, and Ezra Pound and James Joyce in 1920. Hemingway soon learned that it was a city that was, in his own words, 'the best organized for a writer to write in that there is'. He felt very fortunate: 'To have come on all this new world of writing, with time to read in a city like Paris where there was a way of living well and working, no matter how poor you were, was like having a great treasure given you'.

Paris was home while he explored many corners of Europe, while he learned his craft. He told composer George Antheil, who lived above the Shakespeare and Company bookstore, that 'unless you have geography, background, you have nothing'. This sense of geography was as important for the novel as for the novelist. Paris in the 1920s — with its landmarks and people and visiting artists — helped form the writer Hemingway. His experience is a paradigm for the young American expatriate artist.

Though Paris would be his home for seven years, journalism and sports took him all over Europe. He interviewed Benito Mussolini in Milan and Georges Clemenceau in the Vendée. One of the journalists whom he met on these trips, William Bird, would later publish his work. On one of his trips Hadley came to join him and lost, at the Gare de Lyon, a case with most of his early manuscripts ('Up in Michigan' and 'My Old Man' survived).

A number of these early stories were set in his boyhood Michigan. Though he recreated in his early short fiction these scenes of youth, he was drawn to more immediate experiences of war and life in Europe. Unlike James Joyce and other writers who had become exiles from their homes, Hemingway did not long devote his fiction to a re-creation of home. His first novel would be set in France and Spain, his second in Italy.

Hemingway loved sports and their test of his strength and manhood. Paris had sports clubs, boxing rings, tennis courts, and arenas for races. He rarely used these sporting places in his fiction, but he confessed in his memoirs that he 'started many stories about bicycle racing'. With Robert McAlmon and William Bird, both American writers and publishers, he took his first trip to Spain in 1923 to witness a bullfight. He took Hadley to Pamplona in July 1923 for its prenatal influence on their unborn child. (He would give the child a middle name of a Spanish bullfighter: Nicanor.)

Hemingway — nearly everyone called him Hem — made friends easily, and he learned the skill (the literary strategy) of ingratiating himself with the right people. When he and Hadley left after their first year and a half — to fulfil a commitment to his editor and for the birth of their baby in Toronto — he numbered Ezra Pound, Sylvia Beach, James Joyce, Gertrude Stein, Robert McAlmon, and William Bird among his friends. Beach, the owner of the Shakespeare and Company bookshop, lent him $100 for boat passage. By this time McAlmon had published *Three Stories and Ten Poems* for his Contract Publishing Company, and Bird had accepted *in our time* (which he printed without capitalization) for publication by the Three Mountains Press.

After the Hemingways returned to Paris in 1924, they moved near Beach, Stein, and Pound to an apartment above the sawmill in rue Notre-Dame-des-Champs. These were important years for his growing literary reputation: he worked on the *Transatlantic Review* with Ford Madox Ford, returned to Spain, and wrote *The Sun Also Rises* (published in the UK as *Fiesta*), a paean to the 'lost generation'. The novel is filled with the places and people he knew in Paris and Pamplona. Much of the authority of *The Sun Also Rises* comes from his detailed knowledge of these places — their terrain, their smells, their moods.

The experience he was collecting in Paris and Europe was transformed into his most fertile period of writing. Just during the seven months after returning from Toronto, where he had resigned from his job with the *Star*, he wrote nine stories, including 'Big Two-Hearted River'. Though he later romanticized his discipline and poverty, he could afford an extra room to work in and trips to Schruns for skiing and to Pamplona for bullfights. He was comfortable enough to write and enjoy life; he was rich in friends. Visiting writers sought his company, including F. Scott Fitzgerald, who met him at the **Dingo Bar (map E)** in 1925.

The Fitzgeralds, who came to France 'to find a new rhythm for our lives', spent two and a half years in Europe in the mid-1920s — less than half that time in Paris. Unlike Hemingway, Fitzgerald had already served his literary apprenticeship when he came to Paris. He had published five books, yet during the first year he seemed stimulated to create: he wrote *The Great Gatsby* on the Riviera that first summer, 'The Rich Boy' the following spring in Paris, and that autumn he began the first version of *Tender is the Night*. After that his productivity decidedly waned. Paris did give him the setting for three short stories, all written later in Switzerland ('Babylon Revisited', 'The Bridal Party', and 'News of Paris, Fifteen Years Ago'), as well as the second half of Book One of *Tender is the Night*. There are brief Paris scenes in about six other stories. His treatment of Paris summons mood and nostalgia and evokes the senses — the quality of light, the colour of the evening. His topography, though limited, is true and precise. Hemingway's treatment of Paris, though not without error, is both broader and more detailed, and more realistically evocative of place — from the poor neighbourhood of the Place de la Contrescarpe to the bustling cafés of Montparnasse and the sporting fields of the suburbs.

Among Hemingway's friends of the mid 1920s, in addition to Fitzgerald, were John Dos Passos, the Archibald MacLeishes, and the Murphys. Sara and Gerald Murphy — she was an heiress from Ohio and he the son of a New York businessman who owned Mark Cross leather goods — always kept a home in Paris which they lent to the Fitzgeralds and others. The Murphys introduced Hemingway to their rich Riviera life (*Living Well is the Best Revenge* tells their story). In his memoirs, Hemingway blames them and the wealthy Pauline Pfeiffer for the end of his marriage to Hadley: 'then you have the rich and nothing is ever as it was again'.

During the final rewriting of *The Sun Also Rises*, Hemingway's marriage to Hadley disintegrated because he was having an affair with Pauline Pfeiffer, whom he married in May 1927. Though he began writing *A Farewell to Arms* in Paris in March 1928, he was spending more time away from the city. His last Paris address was rue Férou, near Saint-Sulpice, where he lived with Pauline. When he left Paris after nearly seven years, he had completed his apprenticeship. He left having written novels that reworked (purged) and fictionalized (mythologized) the two periods of his apprenticeship, written in reverse order: *A Farewell to Arms* (1929), his war experience in Italy, and *The Sun Also Rises* (1926), his Paris youth. In the words of Roger Asselineau (Europe's leading Hemingway authority), Paris had been 'his university in the same way as a whaling-ship was Melville's Yale and Harvard'.

In the 1930s, when he was feeling mature and was more interested in Montana and Idaho than in France, he told *Esquire* that Paris 'was a fine place to be quite young in and . . . a necessary part of a man's education . . . But she is like a mistress who does not grow old and she has other lovers now'. Yet he would continue to return to Paris (as a rich tourist) for two more decades: to and from an African safari in 1934; with Martha Gellhorn, who would become his third wife, during the Spanish Civil War in 1937–8; at the liberation of Paris in 1944; for the wedding of his son Jack in 1949; and for several short visits in the 1950s before his suicide on 2 July 1961. At his death, French television commemorated his passing by gathering three representatives of his colourful artistic and social life in Europe: Sylvia Beach, the bartender at the Ritz, and a bullfighter.

In the final years Hemingway wrote, 'there is never any ending to Paris and the memory of each person who has lived in it differs from that of any other. We always returned to it . . . Paris was always worth it and you received return for whatever you brought to it.' Today, because his words and his favourite places remain, the visitor can bring Hemingway's memories to his own experience of Paris.

Hemingway described the streets and scenes that follow through different frames — sitting by a yellow tree in Africa, standing in front of his tall desk in Idaho, sitting at a table in a Paris café. These dimensions of time and place influenced his portrait of Paris — portraits that appear in *The Sun Also Rises, In Our Time*, 'The Snows of Kilimanjaro', *A Moveable Feast, Islands in the Stream* — as well as in his nonfiction news articles for the *Toronto Star Weekly*. For example, he wrote *The Sun Also Rises* both within and without, moving in the scene as participant and standing back as immediate observer. From Idaho, decades later, his cinematic frames of Paris are filtered through the lens of memory — the memory of a man who had lost or was losing the gift of writing and was looking back to recreate the experiences that gave birth to that gift.

Because this book is organized according to the topography of Paris,

I will make no attempt to illustrate his changing descriptions of Paris, though they may be observed by the careful reader. In the early fiction, such as in *The Sun Also Rises*, the details of place serve as the tip of an iceberg, the concrete facts that imply or suggest idea and emotion beneath the surface. By the time of his memoirs, the details of Paris places are more panoramic, touched with nostalgia — they are the details of personal myth.

Tracing Hemingway's steps and his fictional settings in Paris has been complicated by several factors: repeated errors that persist even in otherwise reliable biographies, hastily composed guidebooks, and the persistence of Hemingway legends. A few of the legends are repeated here, but they are so labelled. Hemingway himself is responsible for this latter problem. As Michael Reynolds, his latest biographer, points out, 'Early in his career, Hemingway began revising and editing what would become his longest and most well known work: the legend of his life'.

# 2

# HEMINGWAY'S ARRIVAL: SAINT-GERMAIN

The streets sing, the stones talk. The houses drip history, glory, romance.

Henry Miller, in Hôtel Saint-Germain-des-Prés

It was to the 6th arrondissement (6e) of Paris that Hemingway came when he arrived in the city with his bride, Hadley, in December 1921. They checked into a hotel that Sherwood Anderson had recommended. In this arrondissement, near the **Luxembourg Gardens (map C)**, he also rented his final home in Paris — an elegant flat that he shared with his second bride, Pauline. He loved this old section of Paris both when he was a young reporter for the *Toronto Star* and when he was a successful American novelist.

This district near the Seine had been for centuries the home of painters, art schools and galleries, and licensed houses of prostitution. Because there were at least 40 bordellos (before 1945) in the northern portion of the 6th arrondissement, street walkers were rare. This was a district of artists and artists' cafés. Here lived Gertrude Stein, Natalie Barney, Pablo Picasso, Janet Flanner, and, briefly, Ezra Pound and James Joyce, to name just a few. Stein and Pound were Hemingway's two mentors during these early years of his Paris apprenticeship.

In this quarter also are two Left Bank residences (not marked) of the wealthy socialites Harry and Caresse Crosby, who moved to Paris from Boston in 1922. They maintained an apartment at 23 Quai des Grands-Augustins at one time and at another rented a large, three-floor residence at 19 rue de Lille. Their Black Sun Press was located at 2 rue Cardinale, just off Place Furstenberg. From here, in 1931 and 1932, Caresse Crosby would publish an inexpensive continental edition of Hemingway's *Torrents of Spring* and a limited deluxe edition of *In Our Time*.

The streets of this district hold Hemingway's first impressions of Paris. To them he brought his youthful enthusiasm and his dreams of being a writer. 'Paris was always worth it', he would write 30 years later.

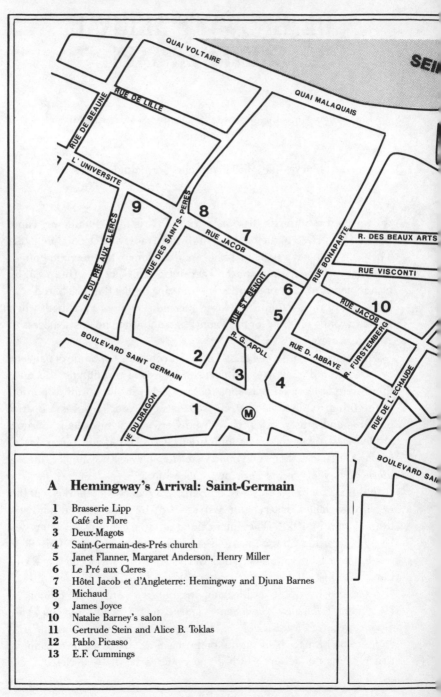

A **Hemingway's Arrival: Saint-Germain**

1 Brasserie Lipp
2 Café de Flore
3 Deux-Magots
4 Saint-Germain-des-Prés church
5 Janet Flanner, Margaret Anderson, Henry Miller
6 Le Pré aux Cleres
7 Hôtel Jacob et d'Angleterre: Hemingway and Djuna Barnes
8 Michaud
9 James Joyce
10 Natalie Barney's salon
11 Gertrude Stein and Alice B. Toklas
12 Pablo Picasso
13 E.F. Cummings

**Métro:** Saint-Germain-des-Prés
**Bus:** 39, 63, 70, 87, 95, or 96

When you leave the métro or get off the bus, look for the major intersection. Brasserie Lipp is diagonally across the street from the church and next to the chemist (look for the sign of the beer mug above the awning of Lipp's).

Hemingway loved the beer and the potatoes in oil at the Brasserie
Lipp.

## 1 Brasserie Lipp: 151 Boulevard Saint-Germain 6e

Paris for Hemingway was not always a moveable feast. Sometimes it was
a fast. He liked to think that his perceptions were heightened by an empty
stomach. 'Hunger was good discipline,' he said, 'I learned to understand
Cézanne much better and to see truly how he made landscapes when
I was hungry.' Later he would romanticize it as poverty. During one such
fast, Hemingway stopped by the **Shakespeare and Company bookshop
(map B)**, where Sylvia Beach urged him to take better care of himself
by going immediately for lunch. He walked to Brasserie Lipp, just off the
Place Saint-Germain-des-Prés:

> There were few people in the *brasserie* and when I sat down on the
> bench against the wall with the mirror in back and . . . I asked for
> a big glass mug that held a liter, and for potato salad.
> The beer was very cold and wonderful to drink. The *pommes
> à l'huile* were firm and marinated and the olive oil delicious.
> I ground black pepper over the potatoes and moistened the
> bread in the olive oil. After the first heavy draft of beer I drank
> and ate very slowly. When the *pommes à l'huile* were gone I
> ordered another serving and a *cervelas*. This was a sausage like a

heavy, wide frankfurter split in two and covered with a special mustard sauce.

I mopped up all the oil and all of the sauce with bread and drank the beer slowly until it began to lose its coldness and then I finished it and ordered a *demi* and watched it drawn.

After this Alsatian meal (*brasserie* originally meant beerhouse) he headed to the **Closerie des Lilas (map E)**, where he sat in a corner with the light over his shoulder and began writing 'Big Two-Hearted River'. In Brasserie Lipp the mirrors, mosaics, menu (and sausage) still await your visit today — at considerably higher prices.

Hemingway was a writer inspired by the ambience, and sometimes by the food and drink, of a quiet café. In a café environment he could write; occasionally he set his fictional scenes here. As in this lunch at Lipp's, his memoirs recreate his love of the Paris cafés. Nearly every page of

Lipp's now has an enclosed terrace and higher prices.

*A Moveable Feast* refers to eating and drinking. Dr Clarence Hemingway, who did most of the cooking for his large family, had taught his son Ernest to appreciate new tastes.

John Dos Passos remembers eating here with the Hemingways in 1922, 'and Ernest's talking beautifully about some international conference he'd recently attended'. The two men, whose friendship was just beginning, discussed their first meeting in Schio, Italy, in May 1918 — a meeting they only vaguely remembered. Unlike Hemingway, Dos Passos had already published several books. Hadley noted that they shared an enthusiasm for physical activity (Dos Passos hiked around Europe) and blindness in one eye.

Across the busy boulevard are two other cafés still famous for their artistic clientele (but more touristy today). A *café-crème* at the Deux-Magots cost about £1.70 in 1988, but the view is worth it.

## 2 and 3  Café de Flore and Deux-Magots: Place Saint-Germain-des-Prés                                      6e

Morley Callaghan, a young Canadian short-story writer and Hemingway's boxing partner in the summer of 1926, calls these cafés 'a focal point,

Café de Flore, corner of rue Saint-Benoît and Boulevard Saint-Germain, has been serving drinks to artists and others since 1865.
(*Robert E. Gajdusek*)

Hemingway preferred the Deux-Magots for 'serious talks'. Opened in 1875, this literary café is the centre of Saint-Germain-des-Prés life.

the real Paris for illustrious intellectuals . . . André Gide might be having dinner at the Deux-Magots. Picasso had often passed on the street.' Samuel Putnam (*Paris was our Mistress*) called Deux-Magots 'neutral ground between warring camps', between Left and Right Banks. Janet Flanner (see Site No. 5) claims that Hemingway preferred the Deux-Magots, now with its green awnings and gold lettering, for 'serious talks'; there they discussed the suicides of their fathers, a tragedy both writers experienced during their 20s. Hemingway remembered drinking also with James Joyce at the Deux-Magots.

Deux-Magots has been a favourite of American artists for decades. Djuna Barnes drank here because she lived for several years just up the boulevard at No. 173. In the autumn of 1929 Allen Tate and Ford Madox Ford spent two or three evenings a week playing dominoes here and at

The two Chinese dignitaries ('deux magots') inside the café named after them. Hemingway and James Joyce drank dry sherry here.

**Closerie des Lilas (map E).** By the mid 1930s André Breton and his band of Surrealists had made this their favourite place.

Café de Flore would be made famous by the Existentialist movement in the 1940s and 1950s. In the 1920s, Hemingway visited Café de Flore (now with cream-coloured awnings and green-and-gold lettering) less than the others, preferring Deux-Magots for his meeting place and Lipp's for its Alsatian cuisine. 'If you really like beer, you'd be at Lipp's', declares Pascin, a Bulgarian painter, to Ernest in *A Moveable Feast*.

Hemingway was a keen observer of people and street life. Today, the Place Saint-Germain-des-Prés is still, especially on a warm afternoon or evening, the centre of village life. Its openness was subdued by the placing of shrubs around the farther pavement terrace of the Deux Magots in 1987. The café clientele and a piece of modern sculpture remind us of how international this 'village' truly is.

Diagonally across from the Deux-Magots is the fountain (*Embâcle*), given recently by the Province of Quebec. This work of art, centrepiece for the Place du Québec, seems to be bursting from the pavement.

Hemingway, who arrived in Paris as a news reporter for a Canadian paper, was also a visitor of churches, and the church of Saint-Germain-des-Prés provides quiet sanctuary from the street activity. The cobblestones extend from the Deux-Magots to the steps of the church.

## 4  Saint-Germain-des-Prés Church                                       6e

This is one of the oldest churches in Paris, built as a monastery chapel. Fragments from the chapel in the park beside it are all that remains of the famous Benedictine abbey, first built in the eighth century. Note the Picasso sculpture *Homage to Apollinaire* in the square near rue de l'Abbaye.

Diagonally across from the small garden of the church and its Picasso sculpture is rue Bonaparte, which takes you toward rue Jacob and Hemingway's first stop in Paris. Halfway down the first block you will see a hotel on the left.

Saint Germain-des-Prés church. In the foreground is the pavement sculpture and fountain given to the city of Paris by the Province of Quebec.

## 5   Janet Flanner, Margaret Anderson, Henry Miller:
36 rue Bonaparte                                                    6e

Hemingway frequently dropped by to see his close friend and fellow journalist Janet Flanner in Hôtel Saint-Germain-des-Prés. Hemingway was from Illinois, Flanner from Indiana, and they would remain steadfast friends. She liked to match wits with him, and she thought that 'by temperament he was professionally excessive, like a form of generosity'.

Flanner moved into the eighteenth-century hotel in 1925 with her companion Solita Solano. There were 19 small rooms (one bath); Flanner and Solano had rooms 15 and 16 (later 13 as well). Jean Cocteau, the French poet, later held his levitations and smoked opium in room 6.

Flanner, who had prominent facial features and an independent mind, was the author of one novel, *The Cubical City* (1926). Under the *nom de plume* 'Genet', chosen for her by her editor Harold Ross, she published her fortnightly 'Letter from Paris' in the *New Yorker*. The first letter was written here and published 10 October 1925. Her last letter was published in 1975 after her return to New York when she was 83 years old. Flanner lived for about 13 years (until 1938) in this small hotel, just a few steps north of the Place Saint-Germain-des-Prés. She later remembered that at dawn she could hear from her bed the singing of the blackbirds in the old trees at the side of the church of Saint-Germain-des-Prés.

Many other expatriates stopped for a while at this hotel, including Margaret Anderson, Kathryn Hulme, and Henry Miller. Anderson, Jane Heap, and Georgette Leblanc (*Souvenirs* records her 20 years with Maeterlinck) edited the last issue of the *Little Review* here. The *patron* was outraged when he discovered that they got green ink all over the sheets. Hemingway was fond of Anderson, whom he took to the prize fights, but he expressed his dislike of her lover, Leblanc, in the *bal musette* scene in *The Sun Also Rises*, by having Jake Barnes introduce the prostitute with bad teeth as 'my fiancée, Mademoiselle Georgette Leblanc'.

Hulme, a friend of these women and later author of *A Nun's Story*, lived on the first floor: 'I could not envisage Heaven offering more, even including the room's appalling wallpaper — a cacophony of alternating stripes of dingy yellow and bands of faded red roses'.

Henry Miller, who would chronicle the 1930s with *Tropic of Cancer* as Hemingway would the 1920s with *The Sun Also Rises*, stayed at this hotel when he first moved to Paris (at an earlier visit he had stayed at another hotel at No. 24 on·this same street). From his fifth-floor room he wrote to a friend in February 1930:

> I love it here, I want to stay forever. . . . I will write here. I will live and write alone. And each day I will see a little more of Paris, study it, learn it as I would a book. . . . The streets sing, the stones talk. The houses drip history, glory, romance.

A marble plaque records that Auguste Comte, the positivist founder of the 'Religion of Humanity', lived here from 1818 to 1822. Note the original wooden doors.

A few more steps take you to the café at the corner of rue Bonaparte and rue Jacob. Until 1540, a canal ran from this corner to the Seine down what is now rue Bonaparte. The canal connected the moat of the Abbey to the River Seine.

## 6  Le Pré aux Clercs: 30 rue Bonaparte                                6e

The Pré aux Clercs (students' meadow) was Hemingway's first neighbourhood restaurant. Dinner for two his first week in Paris came

Le Pré aux Clercs was Hemingway's neighbourhood restaurant during his first days in Paris. It is at the corner of rue Bonaparte and rue Jacob, just a few steps from his hotel.

to only 12 francs, a bottle of good wine cost about 60 centimes. Today a *café au lait* costs as much as Hemingway's two meals. 'The Restaurant of the Pré aux Clercs at the corner of the Rue Bonaparte and the Rue Jacob is our regular eating place', he wrote to Anderson that first month in Paris. It is no longer a restaurant but an ordinary café.

Turn left onto rue Jacob to find the hotel of many American expatriates, on the right.

## 7 Hôtel Jacob et d'Angleterre: 44 rue Jacob        6e

Upon the recommendation of Sherwood Anderson (who stayed here earlier that year), Ernest and Hadley Hemingway rented a room here in December of 1921 upon their arrival in Paris. The hotel was clean, inexpensive (a two-room suite cost 12 francs a day) and crowded with Americans. Today a suite costs more than £55 following the renovation of several of the rooms in 1988. The name of the hotel has contracted, but the prices have expanded.

In the late eighteenth century, when this house belonged to the British, Benjamin Franklin, John Jay, and John Adams hammered out the details of the treaty here with the British, then moved down the road to larger quarters for an official signing. One of the first nineteenth-century Americans to stay here was Washington Irving, who wrote in his journal in 1805 that his room looked out onto a 'handsome little garden'. The nineteenth-century staircase remains, as does the lovely small inner garden, now beautified with glass partitions.

By 1922 a 'flock' of American expatriates had 'descended' on this hotel, according to one of the number. 'Vicki Baum's Grand Hotel' in Greenwich Village (where most of them had come from) 'couldn't touch the drama and intrigue which occurred' here. Among the group were Alfred and Dorothy Kreymborg, Harold Loeb (they published *Broom* 1921–4), Djuna Barnes (*Nightwood*, 1936), and their friends who had worked for the Washington Square Bookshop and various newspapers and magazines. The *Broom* crowd 'meant to be literary at all costs', an observer noted. 'How that little group of pilgrim expatriates loved each other.'

Djuna Barnes moved from Greenwich Village to this hotel just months before Hemingway, who was impressed with her reputation as a lesbian. He wrote one of the first expatriate descriptions of lesbianism in 'The Sea Change', published in Edward Titus's *This Quarter*. In this short story a man and a woman are talking in the Dingo bar, and the implication is that she has developed a lesbian relationship:

Washington Irving,
Sherwood Anderson,
Djuna Barnes, Ernest
and Hadley Heming-
way and dozens of
other American writers
made the Hôtel Jacob
et d'Angleterre their
first stop in Paris.

— I'm sorry, she said.
— If it was a man —
— Don't say that. It wouldn't be a man, You know that . . .

As you leave, notice the original wooden doors on either side of the entry. Continue up ('up' in terms of higher numbers) rue Jacob toward the first intersection. Before the intersection you will see No. 52, where Benjamin Franklin lived with his two grandsons in 1777 before moving to Passy for 8 years, and No. 56 (with a plaque) on the right where, on 3 September 1783, **Franklin, Jay, and Adams signed the peace treaty** with England, recognizing the independence of the United States (see **map G**). Across the street is a very ugly building of the school of medicine for the University of Paris.

**8 Michaud** (now Brasserie l'Escorailles):
corner of rue Jacob and rue des Saints-Pères 6e

Lewis Galantière, a young American (living at the Hôtel Jacob et d'Angleterre) who worked for the International Chamber of Congress and to whom Sherwood Anderson had recommended Hemingway, took Hadley and Ernest to an excellent meal here during their first month in Paris. It was the best meal since their **Café de la Paix crisis (map F)**, in which they did not have enough money to pay the bill. Michaud was a restaurant run by Monsieur Raulo of Brittany, who did the cooking himself.

Within two months Hemingway wrote to Sherwood Anderson and described how James Joyce and 'the whole celtic crew' dined nightly at Michaud. Joyce was then living at 9 rue de l'Université, just across and down the street. Hemingway mentions the Joyce family again in *A Moveable Feast*, where he describes the hunger he and Hadley felt before the 'wonderful meal at Michaud's'.

Harold Loeb, who first came to Paris in 1920 (and stayed at Hôtel Jacob et d'Angleterre), would become a friend of Hemingway. Loeb, the prototype of Robert Cohn in *The Sun Also Rises*, describes Michaud:

> I began to savor Paris as a place in which to live. Down the street a small restaurant, the Café Michaud, simple and unpretentious, served up *haricots verts, petits pois*, new potatoes and *fraises des bois* with a freshness and a delicacy unknown in the United States by those who do not grow their own. And you could go at nearly any hour and meet someone you know at the cafes.

Michaud was the scene of a lunch (probably in 1929) between Fitzgerald and Hemingway, which the latter recounts in *A Moveable Feast*. Hemingway devotes three chapters of his memoirs to making Fitzgerald look fragile, careless, drunken, and uneasy about his sexual adequacy — the last image presented in 'A Matter of Measurement'. Apparently Scott recounted a complaint by Zelda that his penis was too small to satisfy her. After a trip to the toilet and a check of Scott's anatomy, Hemingway pronounced the organ normal. Check the nude male statues at the Louvre, he reassured his worried friend. One unconfirmed story says that they crossed the river to the museum together. This indiscreet admission by Fitzgerald had damaged him in the eyes of Hemingway, who may have fabricated part of this story.

By 1934, when Hemingway could afford an African safari and the best dining, he took Solito Solano, Janet Flanner, and James Joyce to lunch at Michaud, now a run-of-the-mill brasserie. Solano describes Hemingway watching Joyce during the meal 'in a stupor of silent worship'.

In a scene in F. Scott Fitzgerald's *Tender is the Night*, Nicole and Rosemary take a taxi down the rue des Saints-Pères. While they talk about having lived in the street briefly when they were young, Fitzgerald describes the street as looking like 'two dingy fronts [that] stared at them, gray echoes of girlhood'.

Walk a block up rue de l'Université. You will see the Hôtel Lenox sign on your left.

## 9   James Joyce: 9 rue de l'Université                                    7e

The Irish novelist lived here on three separate occasions: one week in July 1920, all of November 1920, and again from 1 October 1921 to 19 October 1922. This later, lengthier stay included the critical months prior to and after the publication of *Ulysses*. Sylvia Beach recruited Hemingway to sell subscriptions for the novel during January 1922. The two men occasionally drank together. Joyce called Hemingway 'a big powerful peasant, as strong as a buffalo', but a sensitive guy; Hemingway admired the frankness of Joyce's great novel, and called the Irishman the 'greatest writer in the world'. At least two critics, Frank O'Connor and Robert Gajdusek, believe that Joyce's work was the most important single influence on Hemingway. One evening, so the story goes, Hemingway took a very drunk Joyce home in a wheelbarrow. The official version is that he carried him 'like a half-empty sack' over his shoulder.

In this same *pension*, T. S. Eliot lived in the autumn of 1910. That winter he attended seven lectures by Henri Bergson at the Collège de France. Eliot later described this at the most romantic year of his life. He was 22 years old. The following July he began working on his poem 'The Love Song of J. Alfred Prufrock', which would be translated for the first time into French by Sylvia Beach and Adrienne Monnier in 1925.

Retrace your steps back to the intersection and continue down rue Jacob. After you pass the short rue Saint-Benoît on the right (Restaurant Chez Papa has no connection with Hemingway), cross rue Bonaparte, scene of many fictional taxi rides from the Left to the Right Bank (see Fitzgerald's *Tender is the Night* and Thomas Wolfe's *Of Time and the River*). If you look up and note the angle of some of the old buildings as you approach

No. 20 on the left, you may look into the room where Colette lived at No. 28.

## 10   Natalie Barney's Salon: 20 rue Jacob                    6e

Pound took Hemingway to visit the Friday afternoon salon of Natalie Barney once in 1922. Although it has long been assumed that the virile Hemingway would have had no commerce with the Barney lesbian world, he was friends with many of the lesbian women of the Left Bank — Stein, Beach, and Flanner in particular. A recent biographer claims that Hemingway, because he was dressed as a girl when he was young, became fascinated with 'the ambiguities of feminine identity', and was 'able in his imagination to identify himself with them'. There is ample evidence that he was attracted to tomboyish or mannish women.

Barney, an American from Ohio, lived for more than 60 years (1909-73) in this seventeenth-century home in the back of the entry courtyard. She entertained the leading writers and intellectuals of many countries and wrote numerous books, chiefly in French. Virtually unknown in her homeland, Barney was a legendary figure in Paris. She is the *Amazone* to whom Rémy de Gourmont addressed his *Lettres à l'Amazone* (1914).

Fitzgerald met Barney through the Murphys, probably in 1927 or 1928, and was invited to one of her 'Fridays'. He keenly observed Barney's guests, which included her current protégée, Dorothy Wilde (niece of Oscar Wilde), and wrote a 20-page manuscript on lesbians in Paris. Barney and Wilde appear as Miss Retchmore and Vivian Taube. Only a few lines of the manuscript found their way into *Tender is the Night* (a scene in which a lesbian propositions Rosemary).

While Fitzgerald directly treated lesbian characters, Hemingway did so indirectly in a 'A Sea of Change' and in the frustrated sexual relationship of two characters in *The Sun Also Rises*: Brett Ashley, the aggressive woman with an androgynous first name and a very short haircut, and Jacob (Jake) Barnes, the impotent hero. According to one biographer, Hemingway derived his hero's name from two prominent lesbians (and their addresses): Natalie Barney, 20 rue Jacob and Djuna Barnes, Hôtel Jacob et d'Angleterre.

As you continue walking down rue Jacob you will see on the right No. 7, where Racine lived with his uncle in 1656, when the future French dramatist was 17 years old. A few more steps and you can look down to the Place Furstenberg, the smallest square in Paris and a favourite of many, including Henry Miller. Just before you reach the park at the beginning of rue Jacob, glance right and you will see up rue de l'Echaudé, a tower of **Saint-Sulpice (map B)**. Rue Jacob is a rare Paris street because it is named after an Old Testament patriarch.

When you have reached the beginning of rue Jacob, turn into the busy market street, rue de Seine. (Raymond Duncan's academy was at No. 31, where George Sand lived in 1831.) Take rue de Buci left to the next intersection. Walk into rue Dauphine just ahead and slightly to the left. The second street on the right is rue Christine. All these narrow streets, in Miller's words, 'drip history, glory, romance'.

## 11    Gertrude Stein and Alice B. Toklas: 5 rue Christine        6e

The Stein/Toklas residence was halfway down in the seventeenth-century building on the right. The outside of the building is virtually unchanged, and wooden mail boxes are inside before you enter the courtyard.

During his early years in Paris, Hemingway did visit the salon of Gertrude Stein in rue de Fleurus. When she and Toklas had to leave their **rue de Fleurus** home **(map D)** in 1938, they moved to rue Christine with their 131 canvasses. By then Hemingway was paying only brief visits to Paris and was no longer one of her devoted circle. Alice Toklas, who never liked Hemingway, lived here until three years before her death in 1967.

Across the street is a good film theatre devoted to the classics. Around the corner to the left was Picasso's studio, on the right.

## 12    Pablo Picasso: 7 rue des Grands-Augustins        6e

Hemingway apparently visited Picasso here before the Second World War. Françoise Gilot, Picasso's mistress, remembers the burly American arriving at the gate of the Spanish painter immediately after the Liberation of Paris:

> One of the first effects of the Liberation was the arrival of Hemingway at . . . rue des Grands-Augustins. Pablo [was away] . . . The concierge in Pablo's building was a very timid woman but not at all bashful. She had no idea who Hemingway was but she had been used to having many of Pablo's friends and admirers leave gifts for him when they called in his absence. From time to time South American friends of his had sent him such things as hams so that he could eat a little better than the average during the war. In fact Pablo had more than once shared food parcels with her.

When she told Hemingway that Pablo was not there and Hemingway said he'd like to leave a message for him, she asked him — so she told us later — 'Wouldn't you perhaps like to leave a gift for Monsieur?' Hemingway said that he hadn't thought about it before but perhaps it was a good idea. He went out to his jeep and brought back a case of hand grenades. He set it down inside her *loge* and marked it 'To Picasso from Hemingway'.

Picasso began working in this studio in the spring of 1936, where he painted 'Guernica', in honour of the suffering of that Spanish city, destroyed in 1937. Later he moved his residence here. After 1955 he lived permanently in southern France.

With your back to the river, walk back up the narrow, curving rue des Grands-Augustins to the end, then turn left at rue Saint-André-des-Arts. Past the police station to the left is No. 46, with the floral iron balconies.

## 13 E. E. Cummings: 46 rue Saint-André-des-Arts          6e

Here in this narrow, crowded street is one of the several addresses (located between two bookshops) of E. E. Cummings. The Massachusetts poet spent most of 1921 to 1923 in Paris and France — returning in 1924, then visiting, sometimes on only brief stops, from 1926 to 1960. His most memorable experience in France occurred in 1917 when he spent several months in detention camp with his friend William Slater Brown, because they were not sufficiently supportive of the French war effort (the charge was based on letters Brown had written). This imprisonment served for his first book, *The Enormous Room* (1922), a modern and ironic version of John Bunyan's *Pilgrim's Progress* (1678). Hemingway called it 'a really fine book', the 'best book' he had read in 1922.

Although Hemingway and Cummings shared the experience of ambulance service during the war and the friendship of Dos Passos, there is little evidence that the midwestern novelist and the ivy-league (MA Harvard) poet enjoyed each other's company.

In *The Twenties: American Writing in the Postwar Decade*, Frederick J. Hoffman says that Cummings's *The Enormous Room* (1922) and Hemingway's *A Farewell to Arms* (1929) 'more than any other [novels], gave the 1920s the most complete rationalization of its postwar attitudes'. Both novels present the individual caught in powerful forces: Hemingway emphasizing individual courage amid the forces of war and nature;

Cummings emphasizing the innocent individual against a corrupt system.

Despite Cummings's imprisonment by the French, he always loved and celebrated Paris as a spiritual place 'continuously expressing the humanness of humanity'. The city is portrayed as a mysterious and sensuous dark lady in poems written in French and English. His poetry, like Hemingway's fiction, appeared in the little magazines *Transatlantic Review* and *This Quarter.* Cummings translated Louis Aragon's poetry into English and was a friend of the French Surrealist poets.

Although Hemingway did not have formal training in French, he was a man who learned by experience — and he absorbed all the experiences of Paris that he could. He talked to shopkeepers, barmen, and the fishermen at the Seine. His hymn to the city is *A Moveable Feast.*

You can end this walk with a drink in the Place Saint-André-des-Arts at the beginning of this street or return up the street to find the **place of Hemingway's most loyal Paris connections (map B)**. Walk west to rue de l'Ancienne-Comédie (where you see Le Conti bar) and turn left. Across from the ancient Le Procope restaurant (note the plaque on the left), you will see the site of the Comédie Française at No. 14. Walk B begins on the other side of busy Boulevard Saint-Germain.

# PLACES OF WORSHIP: ODÉONIA AND SAINT-SULPICE

Turning up from St. Germain to go home past the bottom of the gardens to the Boulevard St. Michel one kept Shakespeare and Company to starboard and Adrienne Monnier's Amis des Livres to port, and felt, as one rose with the tide toward the theatre, that one had passed the gates of dream — though which was horn and which was ivory, neither of those two rare friends would ever undertake to say. Why should they? It was enough for a confused young lawyer in a grand and vivid time to look from one side to the other and say to himself, as the cold came up from the river, Gide was here on Thursday and on Monday Joyce was there.

Archibald MacLeish, remembering rue de l'Odéon on the death of Sylvia Beach

Lying between the Boulevard Saint-Germain and the Luxembourg Gardens in the 6th arrondissement is Odéonia and the Place Saint-Sulpice. The quarter of the Odéon Theatre, historically a neighbourhood of bookshops, was the home of Sylvia Beach's Shakespeare and Company and Adrienne Monnier's La Maison des Amis des Livres — the central exchange for world literature during the first half of this century and, for the young Hemingway, the houses of worship for modern art. The admiration of Beach and Monnier bolstered the young Hemingway when he was establishing himself as a writer. Though both bookshops are gone now, a visit to Odéonia may help you capture a sense of the literary excitement of this quarter. Monnier coined the name Odéonia to identify both this place literally and its larger spiritual boundaries — that country of books and lovers of the word.

Just off the Place Saint-Sulpice, about two blocks west of rue de l'Odéon, Hemingway lived in his third and final home — with Pauline, his second wife. He lived around the corner from his favourite church. In the other direction he could look from his house up the street to the Museum of the Luxembourg, which he had haunted during his first months in Paris. In this museum he studied the paintings of Cézanne. In 1929, in a Nick Adams fragment ('On Writing'), unpublished in his lifetime, Hemingway praises the French painter: 'He was the greatest . . . Nick wanted to write about country so it would be there like Cézanne had done it in painting'. Nick, fishing, recalls his visits to the Cézannes in the Luxembourg and 'knew just how Cézanne would paint this stretch of river'.

This district was also the region of the only two homes on the Left Bank of Zelda and Scott Fitzgerald. The Fitzgeralds were never long-term visitors to Paris, preferring the Riviera. On their first visit to Paris in 1925 (May–July; September–December), they remained chiefly on the moneyed Right Bank. Scott did visit the Hemingways in their second apartment in **rue Notre-Dame-des-Champs (map E)**. His drunken entry, punctuated by his urinating on the steps, caused Ernest a great deal of trouble with his concierge. During the second Fitzgerald visit to Paris (April–August 1928), they discovered the particular excitement of the older and artistic side of the Seine and decided to live across from the Luxembourg Gardens. Key places for Zelda and Scott Fitzgerald are clearly marked on the map that follows.

The 6th arrondissement, covered by maps A, B, and part of C, was the centre of Hemingway's Paris life in the 1920s. He made two of his three residences here, where he had easy access to the Cézanne paintings in the Luxembourg, the books and little magazines in Shakespeare and Company, and the bars and cafés of the Saint-Germain and the Montparnasse quarters.

## 1   La Maison des Amis des Livres: 7 rue de l'Odéon            6e

Hemingway was just learning to make his way around the cold, windswept streets of the 6th arrondissement (6e) in December 1921, when he sought rue de l'Odéon. Sherwood Anderson had given him several letters of introduction — one to an American bookshop on this street — when he told young Hemingway that he had to go to Paris if he wanted to be a serious artist. Because Anderson had dined with Beach and Monnier, Hemingway undoubtedly knew from him that there were two bookshops in rue de l'Odéon. Hemingway probably walked from the Hôtel Jacob et d'Angleterre, through the narrow streets of Saint-Germain to Boulevard Saint-Germain and turned right when he saw the Théâtre de l'Odéon up the street.

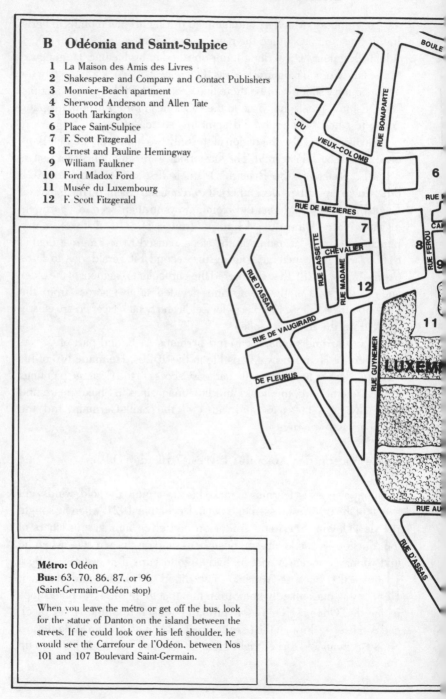

**B  Odéonia and Saint-Sulpice**

1  La Maison des Amis des Livres
2  Shakespeare and Company and Contact Publishers
3  Monnier–Beach apartment
4  Sherwood Anderson and Allen Tate
5  Booth Tarkington
6  Place Saint-Sulpice
7  F. Scott Fitzgerald
8  Ernest and Pauline Hemingway
9  William Faulkner
10  Ford Madox Ford
11  Musée du Luxembourg
12  F. Scott Fitzgerald

**Métro:** Odéon
**Bus:** 63. 70. 86. 87. or 96
(Saint-Germain–Odéon stop)

When you leave the métro or get off the bus, look
for the statue of Danton on the island between the
streets. If he could look over his left shoulder, he
would see the Carrefour de l'Odéon, between Nos
101 and 107 Boulevard Saint-Germain.

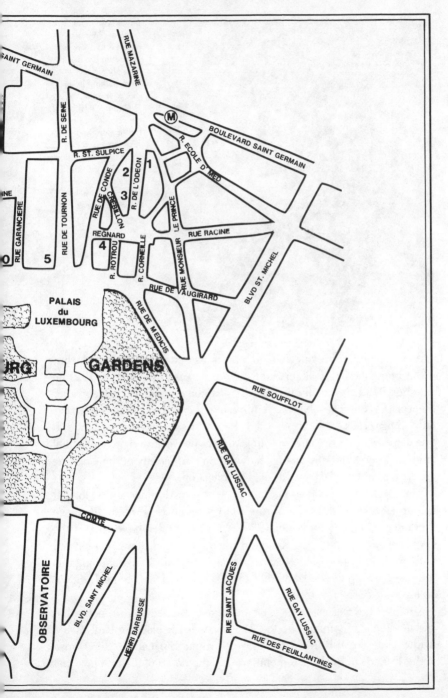

James Joyce and Adrienne Monnier pictured in a wrought-iron sculpture based on a photograph of them walking in this spot in front of the site of Monnier's House of the Friends of Books. Hemingway sold subscriptions for Joyce's *Ulysses*, which was published just weeks after his arrival in Paris, and helped in the smuggling of the book into the United States.

As he entered Carrefour de l'Odéon, he passed No. 15, where Arthur Moss and Florence Gilliam published *Gargoyle* from August 1921 to October 1922. It was the first English-language review to appear after the war. 'Greenwich Village in Montparnasse', one contributor called the little magazine. Although he had begun visiting Stein's salon and Shakespeare and Company, Hemingway was not yet known in intellectual circles. 'I don't know that gang', he wrote to a friend about the *Gargoyle* group the month after they ceased publication.

The French bookshop and library of Adrienne Monnier was on the left as one enters rue de l'Odéon from the Carrefour de l'Odéon. The site remained as a bookstore until 1987. Walk up the left-hand side of the street and you will see the wrought-iron cut-out ahead. It was made from a photograph of James Joyce and Adrienne Monnier walking along this street. Monnier published the French translation (still the standard edition) of Joyce's *Ulysses* in 1929.

Monnier, a writer and editor, presided over the leading French salon and lending library from 1915 to 1955 — a meeting place for Paul Valéry, André Gide, Léon-Paul Fargue, and the young Surrealists. Her House of the Friends of Books is remembered in the name of the art shop that now occupies the space, Les Amis du Dessin. Monnier believed that Hemingway had 'the true writer's temperament' and published his first story ('Fifty Grand') in French in her *Le Navire d'Argent* in March of 1926. It was an all-American edition containing essays by Whitman, William Carlos Williams, Robert McAlmon, E. E. Cummings, and Hemingway. Though small, it had a prestigious circulation and Hemingway was unknown by the French at the time. Since the Second World War, his influence can be felt in many French novels, such as those of Camus.

Archibald MacLeish, lawyer and poet who would later become Librarian of Congress and an undersecretary of state, remembers taking Hemingway to a French literary afternoon here, where André Gide and Jules Romains among others sat in stiff-backed chairs 'talking as if they had rehearsed all morning'. Hemingway's 'hulking body and artless air and charming smile' soon intimidated Gide, who with the others was watching Hemingway, who 'watched the floor'.

> It was too much for Gide. He dropped the topic, whatever it was, and drew Hemingway aside to explain how he punished his cat. He punished his cat, he said by lifting him up by the scruff of his neck and saying PHT! in his face. Whether Hemingway restrained a desire to hit him, I don't know. I was watching the back of his head.

The only French writer Hemingway befriended at La Maison des Amis des Livres was Jean Prévost, with whom he occasionally boxed. Prévost for a time worked as Monnier's assistant editor. She arranged a lively boxing match between the two young men. Apparently Hemingway broke his finger on Prévost's hard head.

Across the street is No. 12, now unrecognizable with a new façade but once home of Shakespeare and Company, operated by Monnier's companion Sylvia Beach. Beach loved this street leading to the columned theatre that somehow reminded her of the 'colonial houses of Princeton', New Jersey, her home town.

## 2   Shakespeare and Company/Robert McAlmon's Contact Publishing Company: 12 rue de l'Odéon        6e

### Shakespeare and Company
In some of the fondest memories of *A Moveable Feast*, Hemingway describes this haven and shrine:

Adrienne Monnier in front of Sylvia Beach's bookshop and lending library in 1936. Monnier published the first Hemingway short story to appear in French.

On a cold windswept street, this was a warm, cheerful place with a big stove in winter, tables and shelves of books, new books in the window, and photographs on the wall of famous writers both dead and living. . . . and even the dead writers look as though they had really been alive.

Sylvia Beach was the owner and operator of this American bookshop and library (it was to the right of the door to No. 12) which Hemingway visited the week he arrived in Paris. She lent him his first books before he could pay the deposit. He would become her 'best customer', borrowing hundreds of books — Turgenev, Tolstoy, Stendhal, and Flaubert — from the lending library shelves. Here he also met many of his contemporary writer friends, including Ezra Pound, Allen Tate, Thornton Wilder, and James Joyce.

A minister's daughter from Princeton, New Jersey, Beach had opened her bookshop in 1919. When she met Hemingway in December 1921, they became instant friends. She thought he was handsome and Latin looking; he admired her wit and shapely legs. She was publishing James Joyce's *Ulysses*, which appeared on 2 February 1922 — a 'most goddamn wonderful book', Hemingway exclaimed. In addition to selling subscriptions to *Ulysses*, Hemingway later signed the petition against Samuel Roth's piracy of her publication — the first a gesture of friendship to Beach, the second an acknowledgement of the importance of the pioneering role of the novel.

Shakespeare and Company was Hemingway's library, post office, and club house during his first years in Paris. Beach lent him the money so that he and Hadley could return to Toronto for the birth of their child. Upon their return to Paris, Ernest would bring the baby to the shop where Bumby would wait patiently for his Papa to read the latest journals. For nearly two decades Hemingway played an active role in the major literary events of the library. He never quarrelled with Beach and praises her in his memoirs: 'no one that I ever knew was nicer to me'.

Katherine Anne Porter, who has written such classic short fiction as 'Flowering Judas' and 'Noon Wine', recalls that Sylvia Beach introduced her to Hemingway in the bookshop one cold spring day in 1934. He was visiting Paris on his way back to Florida from lion hunting in Africa. Beach made the mistake of calling them 'the two best modern writers'. Immediately the telephone rang and Beach retreated to answer it. Hemingway looked long and hard at Porter, who later called him a 'fraud', then walked out without a word.

Hemingway and T. S. Eliot were the only Americans to join a list of

Sylvia Beach with some members of her company. On the second row above the mirror are, from left to right, John Dos Passos, Hemingway, Archibald MacLeish, and Robert McAlmon. William Carlos Williams is above MacLeish, James Joyce below. (*Gisèle Freund*)

distinguished French men-of-letters who gave readings in 1936-7 for the Friends of Shakespeare and Company — a group organized by André Gide to raise money to save the bookshop. Afraid to appear alone, Hemingway recruited Stephen Spender, a young British poet whom he had met in Spain where both were observing the Spanish Civil War. Before their reading at 9 p.m. on 12 May 1937, Hemingway fortified himself with spirits during a dinner in Adrienne Monnier's apartment. He was truly intimidated by the challenge of reading to an audience that included James Joyce, Stuart Gilbert, Natalie Barney, and the new US Ambassador to France, William Bullitt; French writers, Romains, Maurois, Duhamel, Paulhan, Prévost, Chamson, and Valéry; and two newspaperwomen, Hemingway's longtime chum Janet Flanner and Martha Gellhorn, with whom Hemingway had recently begun an affair in Madrid. He stammered at first, then gulped down some beer and began reading 'Fathers and Sons' from *Winner Take Nothing* (1933).

For his final drama in rue de l'Odéon, its 'liberation' from the Nazis, see site No. 3. Beach was forced by the Nazi occupation to close her bookshop during the last days of 1941. She died upstairs at this address in 1962 at the age of 75.

## Robert McAlmon's Contact Publishing Company

Robert McAlmon, who used the Shakespeare and Company address as well as Beach's sales assistance and her Dijon printer, founded Contact Publishing Company here in the early 1920s. He published Hemingway's first volume, *Three Stories and Ten Poems*, in 1923. McAlmon, who moved to Paris the same year as Hemingway, was the son of an itinerant Presbyterian minister in South Dakota and Minnesota. He had money from his wife, Winifred Ellerman (the British novelist Bryher). He was a good short-story writer, a casual editor, and an important friend to many artists in Paris, including James Joyce. McAlmon spent his money and time in drink and travel. He lived very briefly at 8 rue de l'Odéon, for he kept moving. According to numerous memoirs, including their own, he and Hemingway frequently quarrelled:

> Hemingway was a middle western American [says McAlmon, but] . . . outside my experience. At times he was deliberately hard-boiled, case-hardened, and old; at other times he was the hurt, sensitive boy, deliberately young and naive, wanting to be brave, and somehow on the defensive, suspicions lurking on his peering

analytic glances. . . . He approached a cafe with a small-boy, tough-guy swagger.

Rue de l'Odéon is still a street of bookshops, though none remain at Nos 7 or 12. Continue up the street toward the theatre.

### 3 Monnier-Beach apartment: 18 rue de l'Odéon                    6e

In this fifth-floor apartment, up the grand curving stairway, many an international exchange occurred over Adrienne Monnier's famous chicken dinners. Monnier and Beach (who shared the apartment from 1921 to 1936) entertained Ernest and Hadley Hemingway on more than one occasion. On 27 June 1928, they entertained Fitzgerald, Joyce, and André Chamson at dinner. Fitzgerald, thrilled to meet Joyce, called the evening the Festival of Saint James and a few days later drew a picture of the occasion inside Beach's copy of *The Great Gatsby*.

Hemingway made a dramatic reappearance in rue de l'Odéon toward the end of the Second World War. He was a grey-bearded journalist in uniform and travelling with several jeeps and men. Beach remembers, with some exaggeration, Hemingway's 'liberation' of the street — a memory that has certainly augmented the Hemingway mystique:

There was still a lot of shooting going on in the rue de l'Odéon,

Both Hemingway and Fitzgerald dined with Beach and Monnier in their apartment. After the dinner in which Scott Fitzgerald met Joyce, he drew this picture inside Beach's copy of *The Great Gatsby*. He is kneeling in reverence beside the haloed Joyce. Left to right: Monnier, Lucie and André Chamson, Zelda and Scott Fitzgerald, Joyce, and Beach.

and we were getting tired of it, when one day a string of jeeps came up the street and stopped in front of my house. I heard a deep voice calling: 'Sylvia!'

'It's Hemingway! It's Hemingway!' cried Adrienne. I flew downstairs; we met with a crash; he picked me up and swung me around and kissed me while people on the street and in the windows cheered.

We went up to Adrienne's apartment and sat Hemingway down. He was in battle dress, grimy and bloody. A machine gun clanked on the floor. He asked Adrienne for a piece of soap, and she gave him her last cake. He wanted to know if there was anything he could do for us. We asked him if he could do something about the Nazi snipers on the roof tops in our street, particularly on Adrienne's roof top. He got his company out of the jeeps and took them up to the roof. We heard firing for the last time in the rue de l'Odéon. Hemingway and his men came down again and rode off in their jeeps — 'to liberate,' according to Hemingway 'the cellar at the Ritz.'

When you enter the lovely, curved Place de l'Odéon, you will see to the right side of the theatre a hotel where many visiting writers stayed.

## 4  Sherwood Anderson and Allen Tate: 6 Place de l'Odéon   6e

Hôtel Michelet-Odéon, formerly Hôtel de la Place de l'Odéon, was briefly the home of many visiting American and British artists, including Sherwood Anderson, Roger Sessions, Marsden Hartley, and Allen Tate.

Anderson stayed here probably during his second trip to Paris. He came twice for several months each time, in 1921 and 1926-7. The 44-year-old Ohio novelist was excited when he first arrived in Paris and found his *Winesburg, Ohio* in the window of Shakespeare and Company. Beach took him to met Stein, with whom he formed a long-term friendship. This second trip to Paris was marred by ill health and certainly the disappointment of Hemingway's betrayal. Hemingway wrote *Torrents of Spring* in 1925, a parody of Anderson's *Dark Laughter.* In the latter's novel, Esther expresses an attitude typical of many American visitors:

We Americans are considered fools by most Europeans just because there are things we don't want to know. It's because we are from a new country and have a kind of freshness and health in us.

Hemingway occasionally stopped for a drink at the Café
Voltaire after visiting Beach and Monnier in the rue de
l'Odéon, straight ahead. The café, at 1 Place de l'Odéon, was
a favourite haunt of Diderot, Voltaire, Rousseau, Mallarmé,
and Verlaine in their day. (*Roger-Viollet*)

Hemingway made fun of this 'freshness' and sentimentality of his mentor's novel.

Allen Tate, a Kentuckian who would later distinguish himself in poetry and criticism, stayed here from September to December of 1929. During one of his frequent visits to Shakespeare and Company, Sylvia Beach introduced him to Hemingway. They talked briefly, then walked back to the Place and the Café Voltaire at No. 1 (now a library). Here Hemingway took Tate to task for two reviews of Hemingway's work that Tate had written for the *Nation* in 1926. Hemingway then informed Tate that his friend Ford Madox Ford was impotent. Tate recalled this incident in his *Memoirs and Opinions*, which was unfriendly to Hemingway. Though he had praised Hemingway's 'mind of great subtlety and enormous powers of selective observation', after the publication of *A Moveable Feast*, Tate called him a 'son of a bitch' for writing about 'defenselessly dead' friends. 'Ernest Hemingway was handsome and even his malice had a certain charm.'

When the Tates left Paris after their next trip in 1933, Beach and Monnier gave them 'a delightful dinner party', according to Tate: 'all I remember was the warmth and the lively talk, and one remark of Adrienne's: "Monsieur Tate is so conservative that he's almost radical." It was a warning that I hope I have profited by these thirty years.'

Walk down the street (rue Regnard) beside the hotel to rue de Condé. Glance right to see the shorter building with the iron balcony at No. 26, where Beaumarchais, the French dramatist, wrote *The Barber of Seville* in 1775. It has long been the editorial office of the Mercure de France publishing house, with whom Adrienne Monnier had early employment and long ties of friendship. Turn left up rue de Condé and then right into the little park (Square Francis-Poulenc) where you can sit on the bench. You will have the French Senate building (Palais du Luxembourg) in front of you, across rue Vaugirard, and to your right you will see where Booth Tarkington once lived and wrote. You will be sitting on the location of the great Foyot's restaurant, the favourite of writers and politicians for nearly 100 years, but torn down when the street was widened in 1938.

## 5   Booth Tarkington: 20 rue de Tournon                    6e

At the corner of rue de Tournon and rue de Vaugirard, Booth Tarkington, a novelist and short-story writer from Indiana, lived for three years early in the century. 'It was the top number of that wonderful little street', he boasted. Here he wrote 'The Guest of Quesnay' and other stories. He absorbed himself with the history of the street and neighbourhood, including Foyot's across the street. He would point out to visitors that Molière, Balzac, D'Artagnan, and François Villon had all lived near here. Tarkington, who dined at Foyot's regularly, put one of its waiters into two of his stories: 'The Guest of Quesnay' and 'Trois Pigeons'. Though No. 33 is gone, Foyot's remains in the numerous French and English literary works of its patrons.

'Ah! Rue de Tournon!' Tarkington wrote. 'I still haunt the neighborhood in my thoughts of Paris, but the last time I saw it was in 1911, when I went to that corner and looked up at the stone balcony that used to be mine and wondered who was living there — one moonlight night.'

Tarkington was a generation older than Hemingway, but both men wrote about boyhood and adolescence. Hemingway was more influenced by O. Henry and Kipling than by Tarkington who won two Pulitzer Prizes, one for *The Magnificent Ambersons* (1923). A reviewer in 1933 would recommend Hemingway's 'A Day's Wait' to all admirers of Tarkington's *Penrod and Sam*. Tarkington's Penrod tales probably inspired Fitzgerald to write a series of coming-of-age stories about a character named Basil Duke Lee. Fitzgerald, who admired Tarkington's craftsmanship, wrote his own eight stories (1928) with less sentimentality.

Walk one block down rue de Tournon (you will pass, on the right, Casanova's house at No. 27 and John Paul Jones's house at No. 19). Turn left into rue Saint-Sulpice. You will see the church ahead. In the square you may wish to rest at the Café de la Mairie, a café frequented by many writers though the decades, including Djuna Barnes, who set several scenes in *Nightwood* here.

## 6  Place Saint-Sulpice                                                   6e

In *A Moveable Feast*, Hemingway covers essentially the same path you are taking but in the opposite direction. To avoid the smell of

**Below** Café de la Mairie, long a favourite of writers, is located across the Place Saint Sulpice from Hemingway's last home in Paris.

**Right** One of the 'fat belfries', as Henry Miller called them, on the Saint Sulpice church, near Hemingway's home in rue Férou. He and Pauline attended Mass here in 1927–8, as did William Faulkner late in 1926 and Scottie Fitzgerald briefly in 1929.

food and cultivate his hunter-heightened observation, he walks from the Luxembourg Gardens, down 'the narrow rue Férou', through the Place Saint-Sulpice — which he describes as a 'quiet square with its benches and trees . . . a fountain with lions, and pigeons walk[ing] on the pavement and perched on the statues of the bishops' — and on to Shakespeare and Company. He mistakenly remembers that there are 'no restaurants' in the square. Though only a café, the Café de la Mairie, served food and drinks to Hemingway, Fitzgerald, Djuna Barnes, Samuel Beckett, and numerous other writers then and now.

The church of Saint Sulpice where Hemingway attended mass when he lived nearby with Pauline, was his favourite church in Paris. Hotchner claims that Hemingway agreed to say 'a short prayer' there when he was having trouble making love to Pauline shortly after their marriage in 1927. 'Then I went back to my room. Pauline was in bed, waiting. I undressed and got in bed and we made love like we invented it. We never had any trouble again.'

This church, the largest on the Left Bank, is worth a visit. The classical structure (1749) is distinguished on the outside by the massive buttresses and keg-like towers. It is distinguished on the inside by the red marble at the base of the pillars, the statue to Peter ('upon you I will build my church') on the left, and behind the altar the chapel of the Virgin Mary (*Virgin and Child* by Pigalle), probably where Hemingway lighted his candles. The year before Hemingway arrived in the neighbourhood, William Faulkner, who lived nearby, attended Sunday masses here ('Be a good catholic soon', he wrote to his mother).

As you leave the church, walk out toward the street and glance left to see the Hôtel Récamier (No. 3 bis) where Stein and Toklas briefly lived and housed their guests and the hotel that serves as the opening scene of Djuna Barnes's novel *Nightwood*. Barnes describes the hotel as 'neither good nor bad', but 'one of those middle-class hostelries which can be found in almost any corner of Paris'. The rue Palatine is the street running parallel to the church on your left. Across the peaceful square it becomes rue de Mézières. Sit by the fountain and read the next entry.

## 7  F. Scott Fitzgerald: rue de Mézières                    6e

Zelda and Scott Fitzgerald lived in an apartment somewhere in rue de Mézières (or rue Palatine) during April and May of 1929. (They spent the summer on the Riviera.) It was their second residence on the

Left Bank; they had lived for five months the year before in rue Vaugirard — see site No. 12 for his introduction to the Left Bank. Scott's uncontrolled drinking had earned the animosity of Hemingway, who instructed their publisher and his own friends not to reveal to Scott the Hemingway address, which was, ironically, just around the corner. Fitzgerald, who had been expecting to see a lot of Ernest and Pauline Hemingway, was offended by this gesture. Nevertheless, he invited them to dinner in May of 1929:

> Dear Herr Hemophile: or 'Bleeding Boy' as I sometimes call you.
> Will you take salt with us Sun. or Mon. night? would make great personal whoopee on receipt of favorable response. Send me a pneu or answer in person, save between 3 + 7. Highest references, willing to [tra]vel — gens du monde, cultivee, sympathetique cherche hote pour dimanche ou lundi — answer because I shall prob. ask Bishop, if you can come — he is new man without frau.

The tension between the two writers that was generated during this period never completely dissipated. Hemingway did not allow Fitzgerald to see his new manuscript — as he had done with *The Sun Also Rises*. Only when Fitzgerald returned to New York in June did he see *A Farewell to Arms*.

Fitzgerald's French biographer, Le Vot, describes a visit of the Morley Callaghans to this Fitzgerald apartment:

> Once, as they left his apartment building to go to the Café des Deux Magots at Saint-Germain-de-Prés, they crossed the square in front of Saint-Sulpice, Scott's parish church, where Scottie attended mass on Sundays. The Callaghans were also Catholic, but they derided the Saint-Sulpice style of architecture stamped on the neighborhood and thought the church itself was ugly. Scott told them its piers were the most massive in Paris. Curious, they wanted to go inside with him to see them. He stubbornly refused, and when they pressed him for an explanation, he replied, 'Don't ask me about it. It's personal. The Irish Catholic background and all that. You go ahead.'

It was while living in this apartment that Zelda and Scott often quarrelled about Scott's drinking and her accusations about him and Hemingway. Nancy Milford, Zelda's biographer, claims that Zelda overheard Scott talking in his sleep and was convinced that the two men were having a sexual relationship. 'The nearest I ever came to leaving you', he later wrote Zelda, 'was when you told me you [thought] that I was a fairy in the rue Palatine.'

Fitzgerald uses this address in his 'Babylon Revisited', a short story of a father's dissipation and his inability to live down his reputation as a drunk. Charles Wales returned to Paris to visit his daughter, 'Honoria Wales, Rue Palatine, Paris', at the apartment of his sister and brother-in-law. When he leaves the apartment, still hoping to win back custody of his daughter, he is 'trembling'. He walks 'down the rue Bonaparte to the quais', and 'as he crossed the Seine, fresh and new by the quai lamps, he felt exultant'. During his second, disappointing, visit to rue Palatine, he finally realizes the extent to which he had dissipated his life during the 1920s.

Rue Henry-de-Jouvenel — which becomes rue Férou — is on your right as you face the church. The Hemingway apartment is where you see the small Egyptian statue guarding the entrance.

## 8  Ernest and Pauline Hemingway (third home): 6 rue Férou  6e

This apartment of Ernest and Pauline was paid for by her Uncle Gus in 1927. It is on the right going up this picturesque narrow street between the Place Saint-Sulpice and the busy rue de Vaugirard. The street runs into rue de Vaugirard opposite the Musée du Luxembourg, where Hemingway's favourite paintings were then housed. Ada MacLeish helped Pauline (who had been Paris editor of *Vogue*) find the apartment while Hemingway was on a trip (what Pauline called a 'batchelor fling') to Italy with Guy Hickock. The Hemingways lived here in 1927 and 1928, and in April 1929. One can see by the building and the courtyard that this home had a grandeur that his previous Paris residences did not.

At 2 a.m. one morning in March 1928, Ernest pulled a cord that controlled a cracked skylight in the bathroom and the window fell on his head, making a two-inch gash above his right eye. Soon after that, the bandaged head appeared in a publicity picture taken in front of Shakespeare and Company. This photo has been reproduced in numerous books about Hemingway.

Hemingway kept this apartment for some time after he and Pauline moved to Florida. He decided to leave Paris for several reasons, probably including the fact that Hadley had begun seeing Paul Mowrer. He had also accumulated a fair number of enemies on the Left Bank, thanks to *The Sun Also Rises*.

Turn left at the end of rue Férou to find the hotel where William Faulkner lived, just a short block away.

## 9  William Faulkner: 26 rue Servandoni (12 rue de Vaugirard) 6c

Grand Hôtel des Principautés-Unies, with its entrance now on rue de Vaugirard, is where William Faulkner stayed for 20 francs a day from the summer of 1925 until December of that year. His short story 'Elmer' or 'Portrait of Elmer Hodge' is based on this trip to Europe and Paris late in 1925. In a version of the story — probably intended as a novel of an American in Paris — Elmer stays somewhere in rue Servandoni where the landlady, over-worked and scolding, reminds him of his mother. Down to his last resources, Elmer paints a picture in order to be accepted into art school. But in the final section of the story, he has to rush from a café in Montparnasse through the Luxembourg Gardens to the lavatory of his room. While guests wait for him, he sprints to the toilet. After a moment of ecstatic relief, he discovers that there is no toilet paper and reluctantly reaches for his painting. Whether or not Faulkner himself experienced artistic disappointment, loneliness, or financial troubles, is uncertain; but he 'got restless' and stayed only months in Paris instead of the two or three years that he had planned. 'Elmer', which Faulkner pronounced 'not funny enough', was never published.

Faulkner was 29 years old and had published *The Marble Faun*, yet he never tried to meet Beach, Stein, or Hemingway. He later claimed to have gone 'to some effort to go to the café' that Joyce inhabited, but Joyce was 'the only literary man' that he even saw in Paris. He preferred the company of workingmen and children.

During his stay here, when he grew a beard, Faulkner wrote to his mother every Sunday and Wednesday, signing his letters 'Billy': 'I have a nice room just around the corner from the Luxembourg gardens, where I can sit and write and watch the children. Everything in the garden is for children — it's beautiful the way the French love their babies.' By September he had 'come to think of the Luxembourg as my garden' and spent all his time there, writing, sailing boats, and watching the men play 'croquet'.

Richard Le Gallienne had a garret at No. 12 rue Servandoni (the street is named after the designer of the church of Saint Sulpice) where he claimed Charles D'Artagnan of *The Three Musketeers* lodged. Le Gallienne lived in Paris from 1927 to 1935 and wrote a weekly column, 'From a Paris Garret', for the *New York Sun*. Perhaps this is where Faulkner dined nightly at The Three Musketeers restaurant for 25 cents.

Because the building in which Ford lived (No. 21) has been destroyed (you can see the new arcade down the street), you should return to the museum — across the street from rue Férou.

## 10   Ford Madox Ford: 32 rue de Vaugirard                    6e

On the next block up rue de Vaugirard was the apartment building (now gone) where English novelist Ford Madox Ford lived with Stella Bowen. Ford was a friend of Joseph Conrad and Henry James and an important man of letters when he moved to Paris. He held 'Saturday afternoons' at his fourth-floor apartment in the mid 1920s, before he began entertaining at his *Transatlantic Review* offices. When Ford founded the *Transatlantic Review* in 1923, he hoped to duplicate his prestigious *English Review*. Ford entertained Hemingway, whom he admired. Hemingway describes Ford as a man who looked like a walrus and wheezed when he breathed. Their mutual friend Harold Loeb described Ford as being 'blessed with total unrecall'. While at this address Ford published *No Enemy* (1929), an autobiography disguised as fiction, and *Return to Yesterday* (1931), reminiscences.

Allen Tate lived in the Ford apartment for six months in 1929 while Ford was in Toulon. The Harrison Press of Barbara Harrison was also located in this building, replaced by a modern arcade, opposite the Palais du Luxembourg. The new building also claimed No. 30, where Aaron Copland lived in 1921.

## 11   Musée du Luxembourg: 19 rue de Vaugirard                    6e

The Palais du Luxembourg (No. 15) and its museum (No. 19) are where Hemingway went to study the paintings of Manet, Monet, and, particularly, Cézanne: 'I was learning something from the painting of Cézanne that made writing simple true sentences far from enough to make the stories have the dimensions that I was trying to put in them', Hemingway remembered.

The palace, built by Marie de Medici and inspired by the Pitti Palace in Florence, now serves as the seat of the French Senate, and the paintings Hemingway admired in the museum were moved to the Jeu de Paume and in 1986 to the new museum in the old Gare d'Orsay.

the best place to go was the Luxembourg gardens where you saw

Musée du Luxembourg, where Hemingway studied Cézanne's paintings: 'He wanted to write like Cézanne painted'. Taken from the street where Hemingway lived.

and smelled nothing to eat all the way from the Place de l'Observatoire to the rue de Vaugirard. There you could always go into the Luxembourg museum and all the paintings were sharpened and clearer and more beautiful if you were belly-empty, hollow-hungry.

Return across the street and turn left. As you approach rue Bonaparte, the Fitzgerald residence is directly in front of you. Note the Allée du Séminaire, a resting area on the corner.

## 12   F. Scott Fitzgerald: 58 rue de Vaugirard                    6e

Zelda and Scott lived here at the corner of rue Bonaparte and rue de Vaugirard, from April to August of 1928. Their apartment, which faced an inner courtyard and garden, was found for them by Sara and Gerald Murphy, who had often kept an apartment in Paris since 1921 (though they lived chiefly in the south of France). The Murphys were then renting an apartment in a new building just two minutes' walk along the park at No. 14 rue Guynemer. The Murphy children played with Zelda and Scott's daughter Scottie.

In Fitzgerald's *Tender is the Night*, the Divers live here, 'high above the green mass of leaves' of the Luxembourg Gardens. During a luncheon here, Rosemary becomes aware that Dick Diver is falling in love with her.

Fitzgerald, the provocator and spokesman for the 'jazz age', was born in St. Paul, Minnesota, in 1896 (three years before Hemingway's birth). His middle-class parents sent him to private schools and, in 1913, to Princeton, which he left in 1917 to join the army. While stationed in Montgomery, Alabama, he met Zelda Sayre, whom he married (in St. Patrick's Cathedral, New York City) soon after the publication of his first novel, *This Side of Paradise* (1920). Their daughter, Scottie, born in 1921, lived here with them. Scott had already published *The Beautiful and the Damned* (1922) and *The Great Gatsby* (1925) when the Fitzgeralds arrived on the Left Bank.

Fitzgerald's encounter with Paris has been assumed to be more than it was. When he first came to Paris for a long visit in 1925, he stayed on the Right Bank with little contact (except his meeting Hemingway) with the literary community of the Left Bank. It was not until his trip of 1928 that he made a conscious attempt to meet the new writers or the French. Through Sylvia Beach he met his most important French ally, André Chamson, who would write the introduction to the French translation of *The Great Gatsby* and do much for his reputation in France. Scott's letters to Max Perkins from this address express his enthusiasm for Chamson's *Les Hommes de la Route*, a novel Beach suggested to Fitzgerald and King Vidor for a movie. After much Hollywood talk, the plan was abandoned. But Scribner's (Fitzgerald's publishers) published the novel, translated as *The Road*, in 1929.

The Fitzgeralds came to Paris for stimulation; they were, in Zelda's words, 'excitement eaters'. Hemingway called theirs a 'festival conception of life'. The Fitzgeralds thought that they were more sophisticated and open to Europe than their fellow travelling citizens. Scott told a reporter for the *New York World* that 'France has the only two things toward which we drift as we grow older — intelligence and good manners'. Yet on occasion he and Zelda exhibited little of either. They played and spent extravagantly and were more comfortable on the sunny Riviera. Fitzgerald's Paris experience was not an enriching period of his life. On the contrary, according to Mizener it 'ended in emotional bankruptcy'. Zelda, who took intensive ballet lessons from Lubor Egorova (with Ballet Russe) during this particular visit, describes Scott as being 'literally eternally drunk the whole summer'.

The expatriate life was a blend of both alcoholic excess, as exemplified in the Fitzgeralds, and serious idealism, as exhibited in the awe with which MacLeish 'passed the gates of dream' into rue de l'Odéon. Hemingway had a capacity for both.

If you continue along the side of the park on rue Guynemer (which begins at the front of the Fitzgerald site) for one block, you will come to rue de Fleurus, where Gertrude Stein lived and where map C begins.

# 4

# GERTRUDE STEIN, THE GARDENS, AND THE RIVER

In the morning I walked down the Boulevard to the rue Soufflot
for coffee and brioche. It was a fine morning. The horse-chestnut
trees in the Luxembourg gardens were in bloom. There was a pleasant
early-morning feeling of a hot day.

Jake Barnes on Boulevard Saint-Michel (*The Sun Also Rises*)

O déonia and the church of Saint Sulpice were not the only inspirations
for young Hemingway. Among the most vivid impressions of his early
years in Paris were the stimulation of his conversations with Stein and the
hours of quiet contemplation in the Luxembourg Gardens and along the
*quais* of the Seine.

This third walk in the Paris of Hemingway and Stein will take you from
her famous salon, through the Luxembourg Gardens, along the noisy
Boulevard Saint-Michel (Boul' Mich') and to Notre Dame Cathedral. There
are ideal spots — as there were for the young Illinois writer — to sit and
contemplate. You may wish to begin not at Stein's salon but with a quiet
hour in the gardens. The description of the gardens that follows will give
you a central orientation to the Left Bank of the expatriate literary Paris.

The territory of this map includes the land that linked Hemingway's
Paris destinations — a land of avenues and access. Stein was his link from
newswriting days to the world of letters. The Boul' Mich' linked
Montparnasse cafés to the Right Bank newspaper offices. The Luxembourg
gardens are crisscrossed with his footsteps, for he traversed here going
from his Montparnasse apartment to Sylvia Beach's shop, from Stein's
salon to Ford's *Transatlantic Review* office beyond Notre Dame, and from
his first apartment in Cardinal-Lemoine to Stein's apartment. The
numerous references to his walking through Paris reveal that the territory
of this map was the centre of his Left Bank. Numerous references in the
memoirs of his friends recall meeting Hemingway on the gravel paths of
the gardens.

## 1   Gertrude Stein: 27 rue de Fleurus                          6e

Rue de Fleurus was made famous by Gertrude Stein, who bears the rare distinction among American and English writers of having a plaque mark her former residence, just two and a half short blocks from the gardens. With the exception of Edith Wharton in the rue de Varenne, Stein possessed grander lodgings than most other expatriate writers, especially Hemingway. She shared with Toklas (they were both from California) the ground-floor apartment to the right of the garden courtyard. Stein wrote every day, disliked revision, and was frustrated by a lack of acceptance of her writing. Nevertheless, American writers often sought an audience with her, brought, as in the case of Sherwood Anderson, by Sylvia Beach.

When Hemingway first visited her in March 1922, he passed through double doors to what James R. Mellow calls 'a ministry of propaganda for modern art'. Though the two Americans sat beneath the paintings of

'We loved the big studio with the great paintings', Hemingway said of Gertrude Stein's home in rue de Fleurus. Only a portion of the courtyard apartment is shown through the trees. Stein and Toklas lived in the two floors to the right as well as the corner room ahead.

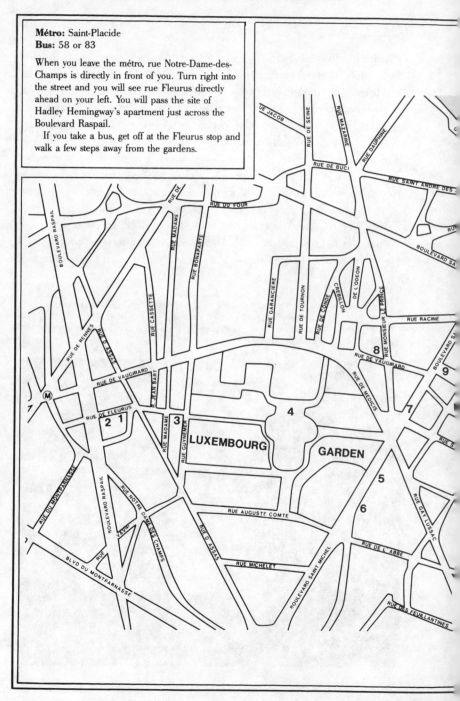

**Métro:** Saint-Placide
**Bus:** 58 or 83

When you leave the métro, rue Notre-Dame-des-Champs is directly in front of you. Turn right into the street and you will see rue Fleurus directly ahead on your left. You will pass the site of Hadley Hemingway's apartment just across the Boulevard Raspail.

If you take a bus, get off at the Fleurus stop and walk a few steps away from the gardens.

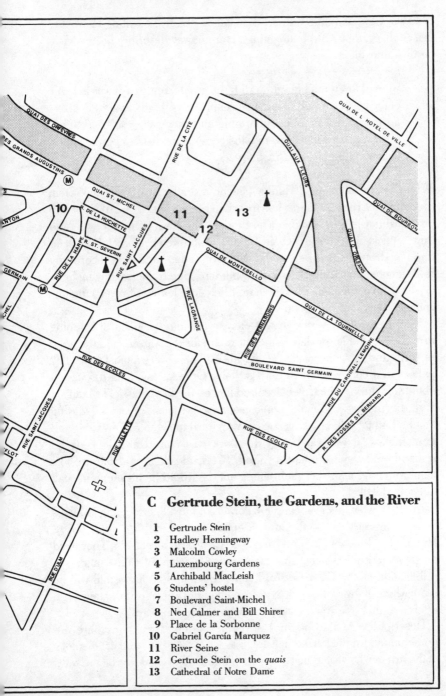

## C  Gertrude Stein, the Gardens, and the River

1   Gertrude Stein
2   Hadley Hemingway
3   Malcolm Cowley
4   Luxembourg Gardens
5   Archibald MacLeish
6   Students' hostel
7   Boulevard Saint-Michel
8   Ned Calmer and Bill Shirer
9   Place de la Sorbonne
10  Gabriel García Márquez
11  River Seine
12  Gertrude Stein on the *quais*
13  Cathedral of Notre Dame

Picasso, Gauguin, and Matisse, they talked chiefly of writing (as well as baseball, gardens, and bullfighting). Hemingway describes his first visits to this apartment:

> we had loved the big studio with the great paintings. It was like one of the best rooms in the finest museum except there was a big fireplace and it was warm and comfortable and they gave you good things to eat and tea and natural distilled liqueurs made from purple plums, yellow plums, or wild raspberries.

While Toklas intercepted Hadley (as she did all wives of writers), Stein entertained Ernest, who was less than half her 48 years. She thought him 'extraordinarily good-looking'; he thought she had 'beautiful eyes' and 'lovely, thick, alive immigrant hair'. Chiefly he admired her forceful character and her strong Yankee personality. She dressed in sandals and corduroy and sang her own song like a Walt Whitman: 'She is the rise having been arisen. She is the lamb and the lion. She is the leaven of reverberation.' Initially, they 'got on famously'.

Hemingway later wrote, 'It was easy to get into the habit of stopping in at 27 rue de Fleurus late in the afternoon for the warmth and the great pictures and the conversation'. He added, 'There were almost never any pauses in a conversation with Miss Stein'. Once after a long discussion about sex, during which Stein lectured him on the happiness of lesbianism and the ugliness of male homosexuality, he was so late in leaving that he had to walk up along rue de Vaugirard to get to rue du Cardinal-Lemoine — 'it was sad when the park was closed and locked', he remembered. Soon he told a friend, 'Gertrude Stein and me are just like brothers'. Later, after their falling out, he would, in his memoirs, call her an 'old bitch'.

In 1925, soon after meeting Fitzgerald and just before going to Lyons to help him retrieve his car (an incident described in *A Moveable Feast*), Hemingway brought Fitzgerald to rue de Fleurus to meet Stein. They liked each other immediately, and Stein wrote a letter of praise after the publication of *The Great Gatsby*. Later she wrote that 'Fitzgerald will be read when many of his well known contemporaries are forgotten' — a reference that both men assumed to be to Hemingway.

Descriptions of the lodgings and the literary discussions here are numerous and sprinkled through the histories of the period and the memoirs of the artists who visited this salon each week. They all describe the walls crowded with paintings, the heavy furniture, and the hushed atmosphere of their encounter with the 'Sibyl of Montparnasse'. One painter observed that visiting her was like going to school.

A Canadian teenager named John 'Buffy' Glassco came uninvited to one of Stein's parties, which he found 'almost ecclesiastical' in atmosphere: 'She awakened in me a feeling of instinctive hostility coupled with a grudging veneration, as if she were a pagan idol in whom I was unable to believe'. During an animated discussion about the virtues of Jane Austen's work, Glassco was joined by Stein.

> 'Do I know you?' she said 'No. I suppose you are just one of those silly young men who admire Jane Austen.' . . .
> 'Yes, I am,' I said. 'And I suppose you are just one of those silly old women who don't.' The fat Buddha-like face did not move. Miss Stein merely turned, like a gun revolving in its turret, and moved imperturbably away.

Glassco was immediately told to leave by a 'tweedy man' and headed for the Dôme, determined never again to go to a party 'without being invited'. He recorded his experience in his memoirs, which he began upon arriving in Paris in 1928.

The strain in the relationship between Stein and Hemingway probably began when he wrote *Torrents of Spring*, a parody of her friend Sherwood Anderson, which included an attack on her. Malcolm Cowley claims he 'couldn't forgive anyone doing him a favour' — and he was indebted to both Anderson and Stein. In her *Autobiography*, she got even for them both by calling Hemingway 'yellow' and claiming that she and Anderson had taught him to write and had introduced him to boxing and bullfighting. He got even years later in the description of an overheard scene of lesbian cruelty upstairs in this Stein apartment. The implication is that the overhearing of this incident led to the break up of the friendship, though undoubtedly he had known about the relationship between Stein and Toklas for years.

In 1938, long after Stein and Hemingway had fallen out, she and Toklas moved from 27 rue de Fleurus to 5 rue Christine, a short, narrow street north of the Carrefour de l'Odéon (discussed on the first Hemingway walk). Though Stein is the most famous American to live in this street, thousands of others have lived and studied here at the Alliance Française and, earlier, at the American University Union (Site No. 3). Elmer Rice, American playwright, lived on this street in 1925 and Allen Tate, American poet, lived here in 1928.

Just two doors up in the midst of what is now the expanded Alliance Française, was the apartment (now gone) of Hadley and Jack 'Bumby' Hemingway.

## 2  Hadley Hemingway: 35 rue de Fleurus                              6e

With Bumby and their cat (Mr Feather Puss), Hadley moved in August of 1926 into a sixth-floor apartment (now gone). She had asked for a trial separation from Hemingway. He was having an affair with Pauline, whom he wished to marry. When Hadley left Ernest, she first lived across from the Closerie des Lilas in the Hôtel Beauvoir, then moved to Stein's street.

When Hadley agreed to divorce, Ernest transported in a wheelbarrow the belongings she chose, including her birthday present of the previous year, Joan Miró's *The Farm*. Their divorce became final on 27 January 1927. 'I did love him', she later acknowledged, 'as though he were a child'. After an extended trip to the United States, she moved to 98 Boulevard Auguste Blanqui (13e), in October 1927. She was then seeing Paul Scott Mowrer, the first foreign correspondent to win the Pulitzer Prize, whom she was to marry in 1933.

The building where she lived was demolished in 1988. It was once the back entrance to the Foyer des Étudiants, in the centre of the Alliance Française, expanded to the new building across the street. The Alliance Française (101 Boulevard Raspail) continues to teach thousands of foreign writers, artists and students.

Turn down rue de Fleurus toward the park. You will pass rue Madame, in which (at No. 58) lived Stein's brother Michael and his wife Sarah, who were also avid art collectors. The last building on the right is No. 1.

## 3  Malcolm Cowley: 1 rue de Fleurus                                 6e

At one time the American University Union, which had 30,000 students enrolled in 1919, was located here. Malcolm Cowley lived here in October 1917 on his way back to Pittsburgh from ambulance and transport driving service, and in July 1921 before journeying to Montpellier for graduate study under an American Field Service fellowship. On 2 July he wrote from here to Kenneth Burke:

Paris is like Cocaine; either it leaves you tremendously elated or sunk in a brown fit of depression. I begin now to understand its fascination, and I subscribe to the opinion of ten thousand Matty Josephsons: You must come to Paris. Only, you mustn't stay here.

In October he published 'The Journey to Paris' in *Gargoyle*, the first expatriate little magazine, published by Arthur Moss and Florence Gilliam in Carrefour de l'Odéon.

Cowley visited Paris during vacations from his studies in Montpellier until 1923. His distance from Paris gave him an objective observation of Modernism, and his study of French Classicism made him more of a Humanist and Realist. Even then Cowley, who would become the spokesman of the American expatriate 1920s, was analysing and writing about his literary generation. Several essays of this period, such as 'A Brief History of Bohemia' (1922), became part of his major work on his generation, *Exiles Return* (1934). His associate editorship of *The New Republic* (in the 1930s) and his *Exiles Return* made his reputation — along with his critical work on William Faulkner and Hemingway.

Cross rue Guynemer and enter the park at the west entrance. A brief history and map of the gardens is on the kiosk to the left beyond the entrance. You will see the fountain ahead as you walk past the tennis courts (left) and the handball court (right).

## 4  Luxembourg Gardens                                              6e

Cowley, Hemingway, Stein, Fitzgerald, and dozens of American expatriates lived within steps of the gardens. Later in life Hemingway described the gardens in *A Moveable Feast* and in *Islands in the Stream*. In this last work, a posthumous novel published in 1970, he gives a panoramic memory that takes in the boats in the pool around the fountain, men bowling, and the gravel paths:

> I can remember the Jardin du Luxembourg well. I can remember afternoons with the boats on the lake by the fountain in the big garden with the trees. The paths through the trees were all gravelled and men played bowling games off to the left under the trees as we went down towards the Palace and there was a clock high up on the Palace. In the fall the leaves came down and I can remember the trees bare and the leaves on the gravel. I like to remember the fall best.

'I can remember the Jardin du Luxembourg well. I can remember afternoons with the boats on the lake by the fountain in the big garden with the trees', wrote Hemingway in *Islands in the Stream*.

. . . the way everything smelled in the fall and the carnivals and the way the gravel was dry on top when everything was damp and the wind on the lake to sail the boats and the wind in the trees that brought the leaves down.

In this novel he fictionalizes killing pigeons by the Medici Fountain at dusk to keep from starving. Hadley confirms this was only fiction.

After the *quais*, Hemingway found the Luxembourg Gardens the most congenial place for strolling. He frequently cut through the paths and by the fountain of this last remaining Renaissance garden in Paris on his way to or from the rue de l'Odéon and the Seine. In March of 1922 he and Hadley walked through the gardens to rue de Fleurus to meet Stein, whom he later often met strolling on the gravel paths of the Luxembourg.

In Henry James's *The Ambassadors*, Lambert Strether pulls up a 'penny chair' and passes an hour 'in which the cup of his impressions seemed truly to overflow'. William Faulkner's *Sanctuary* (1931) concludes with Temple Drake in Paris on 'a gray day, a gray summer, a gray year':

> in the Luxembourg Gardens as Temple and her father passed the women sat knitting in shawls and even the men playing croquet played in coats and capes, and in the sad gloom of the chestnut trees the dry click of balls, the random shouts of children and that quality of autumn, gallant and evanescent and forlorn. From beyond the circle with its spurious Greek balustrade, clotted with movement, filled with a gray light of the same color and texture as the water which the fountain played into the pool, came a steady crash of music. They went on, passed the pool where the children and an old man in shabby brown overcoat sailed toy boats, and entered the trees again and found seats. Immediately an old woman came with decrepit promptitude and collected four sous.

The old women (war widows) no longer collect coins for the privilege of sitting in the chairs of the garden.

If you sit with your back to the Palace (now the French Senate) and with the fountain directly in front of you, you will have your back to the Seine and Hemingway's first, brief residence in Hôtel Jacob et d'Angleterre. To your left beyond the trees is the Latin Quarter, the Panthéon (with the cross on top), and **Hemingway's first apartment** (described in **walk D**). Straight ahead, in line with the fountain, statues, and observatory is the beginning of the Boulevard du Montparnasse and, slightly to the right (in the rue Notre-Dame-des-Champs), **Hemingway's second apartment** (described in **walk E**). In the direction of the Montparnasse Tower (toward the right) was Stein's rue de Fleurus apartment, just past the gates to your right.

To find the Boul' Mich', walk up the stairs to the left (assuming that your back is still to the Senate). You will see the ornate gate to the Boulevard Saint-Michel ahead. To the right up the Boul' Mich' lived many foreign artists, including those in the following sections. If you wish to take this small detour for the next two locations, the beautiful iron-work façade of the student hostel (No. 6) is worth seeing.

## 5   Archibald MacLeish: 85 Boulevard Saint-Michel        6e

MacLeish lived in many locations in Paris during his many visits, but he lived here when he made his very first visit in 1923. He was trained as a lawyer when he arrived that year, but would earn his fame as a poet, dramatist (*J.B.*), and Librarian of Congress. MacLeish, who had a gift for friendship, soon became closely associated with Hemingway, whom he praised for 'the one intrinsic style our language has produced in this century'. MacLeish, Hemingway, Dos Passos, Gerald Murphy, and their wives skied in Austria and sunned themselves on the Riviera. In part because Joyce liked to sing with Ada MacLeish, Archibald was a friend of Joyce; in later years he would send a cheque to Sylvia Beach for a case of white Alsatian wine for Joyce each Christmas.

In later years MacLeish, in an article in the *Saturday Review*, explained and defended his generation in the 1920s as a generation that had been failed by its own country. In the 'greatest period of literary and artistic innovation since the Renaissance', the 'song may have been tragic, but the song itself was new. . . . Not philosophy, not the church, but the painters and poets and composers of those years showed us what and where we were'.

## 6   Students' Hostel: 93 Boulevard Saint-Michel        6e

Here, facing the School of Mines and the Luxembourg Gardens, is the Foyer International des Etudiants (students' hostel), open to students of all nationalities since the First World War. Innumerable students and young would-be artists stayed here during the 1920s.

During the Second World War Sylvia Beach hid here after being released from internment camp, where she spent six months of 1942 (after the United States entered the war against Germany). Beach 'lived happily in the little kitchen at the top of the house' with Miss Sarah Watson (herself interned for a while) and her assistant, Madame Marcelle Fournier. Fournier told me in 1969 that the kitchen sink dripped constantly, though Beach claimed it made her think she was in a Japanese garden. Beach had returned to 18 rue de l'Odéon by 1944 when Hemingway arrived with his jeeps to 'liberate' Odéonia.

The iron- and glass-work on the front of this building make it one of the most beautiful sites on the boulevard. Just a few steps further up the boulevard in Hôtel de l'Univers (now Hôtel de l'Observatoire on the corner) lived Alice B. Toklas in 1907–8, when she was beginning her friendship

Number 93 Boulevard Saint-Michel, serving visiting students from America since the First World War. Sylvia Beach hid on the top floor from the Nazis in 1942.

with Gertrude Stein and they walked in the gardens together. Her room faced the garden of the Institut des Jeunes Sourds (deaf).

As you return down the boulevard toward rue Soufflot (which begins at the Pantheon and ends at the boulevard opposite the fountain), you will be tracing the steps of Jake Barnes in Hemingway's first novel.

## 7  Boulevard Saint-Michel (Boul' Mich')                    5e/6e

In *The Sun Also Rises*, Jake Barnes, who lives in an apartment on the Boul' Mich', describes his walk down to the rue Soufflot for breakfast:

> In the morning I walked down the Boulevard to the rue Soufflot for coffee and brioche. It was a fine morning. The horse-chestnut trees in the Luxembourg gardens were in bloom. There was the pleasant early-morning feeling of a hot day. I read the papers with the coffee and then smoked a cigarette. The flower-women were coming up from the market and arranging their daily stock. Students

went by going up to the law school, or down to the Sorbonne. The Boulevard was busy with trams and people going to work. I got on an S bus and rode down to the Madeleine, standing on the back platform. From the Madeleine I walked along the Boulevard des Capucines to the Opéra, and up to my office.

Where Jake had his brioche and coffee is now probably one of the fast-food establishments that blight the street.

Before entering Place de la Sorbonne, turn left off the Boul' Mich' into rue de Vaugirard, the longest street in Paris. Just around the corner on the left is the Hôtel Trianon Palace, where Richard Wright (author of *Black Boy* and *Native Son*) lived briefly in the 1940s. Number 4 is in the next block on the right.

## 8   Ned Calmer and Bill Shirer: 4 rue de Vaugirard                    6e

Several fellow American journalists of Hemingway lived here in the 1920s in the Hôtel de Lisbonne (now Hôtel Luxembourg). They served as models, as did Hemingway himself, for Jake Barnes. William L. Shirer and Edgar (Ned) Calmer, both newspapermen and friends of Hemingway, left their impressions of the Hôtel de Lisbonne. Shirer praises the spacious rooms, large writing tables and bookcases, but despairs of the hall toilets:

> There was a so-called stand-up toilet by the stairwell on each floor. But it took some practice and a great deal of dexterity to use it. . . . The trick was to achieve a proper balance without keeling over and then, at the end, keeping your balance, to reach high for the nail on the soggy wall from which old cut-up newspapers hung.

Private toilets have since been installed, and the hotel was entirely refurbished in 1981.

Ned Calmer, who wrote a novel about the hotel in 1961 (*All the Summer Days*), lived there for a good part of seven years. When Hemingway discovered in 1933 that Calmer's two-year-old daughter was not baptized he expressed alarm, helped arrange the ceremony, and served as godfather.

## 9   Place de la Sorbonne: 47 Boulevard Saint-Michel                    5e

The hub of student life, this square has seen many renovations, but usually holds bookshops and cafés. At No. 47, at the entrance to the Place de la Sorbonne, was Café d'Harcourt, a popular terrace café in the 1920s frequented by Hemingway, McAlmon, Joyce, and others.

Walk toward the Seine, past the Roman baths and Cluny Museum (on the right) and across Boulevard Saint-Germain. Hemingway takes this walk in his memoirs and stops at a café in the Place Saint-Michel to write a short story and drink two rum St. James's. After finishing the story he orders oysters and white wine: 'After writing a story I was always empty and both sad and happy, as though I had made love'.

## 10  Gabriel García Marquez: Boulevard Saint-Michel          6e

On a rainy spring day in 1957, Gabriel García Marquez (author of *One Hundred Years of Solitude*) saw Hemingway walking on the other side of the street and wearing 'cowboy pants, a plaid shirt and a ballplayer's cap . . . [looking] so alive amid the secondhand bookstalls'. The 28-year-old Colombian, then a newspaperman with one published novel, would one day himself win the Nobel Prize. Instead of spoiling the moment with autograph or effusive praise, Marquez cupped both hands to his mouth and yelled 'Maaaeeestro!' The 59-year-old writer turned, raised his hand, and shouted in Castillian, 'Adiooos, amigo!' This was 'the only time I saw him', recalls Marquez, adding, 'my two great masters were the two North American novelists to have the least in common': Hemingway and Faulkner.

Marquez's recollection may be the last record of Hemingway in the streets of Paris.

Either walk right along the river to the park, or cut through one of the narrow streets before the *quai*: rue Saint-Séverin will take you past the Saint-Julien-le-Pauvre church; rue de la Huchette, made famous in several books by Elliot Paul (*The Last Time I Saw Paris*), will take you to the front of George Whitman's Shakespeare and Company. All three alternatives will take you across rue Saint-Jacques. This medieval quarter has teeming, narrow streets; lovely churches (Saint Julian of the Poor is the oldest and one of the smallest in Paris); and the remarkable Square René-Viviani, next to Saint Julien, with the best view of Notre Dame. Before crossing the Seine one should turn the corner (rue de la Bûcherie) on the left to visit George Whitman's Shakespeare and Company bookshop (so named in 1964), which dates from the 1950s. Rest with a book in the shop (which faces the river) or with the pigeons in the park.

## 11 **River Seine:** Quai de Montebello 6e

Hemingway loved to walk the *quais* and browse the bookstalls. He found English books, discarded from nearby tourist hotels, from the Quai Voltaire to the Quai des Grands Augustins and further on at a bookstall near the Tour d'Argent. He also loved to watch the fishermen, some of whom he knew. Hemingway, who did not own tackle, saved his own fishing experience for Spain. But he wrote with authority about fishing the Seine: 'The good spots to fish changed with the height of the river and fishermen used long, jointed, cane poles but fished with very fine leaders and light gear and quill floats and expertly baited the piece that they fished', he wrote in *A Moveable Feast*. The fish 'were delicious fried whole and I could eat a plateful. They were plump and sweet-fleshed with a finer flavor than fresh sardines even.'

In *By-Line* ('Christmas in Paris'), he exclaims:

> it is wonderful in Paris to stand on a bridge across the Seine looking up through the softly curtaining snow past the grey bulk of the Louvre, up the river spanned by many bridges and bordered by the grey houses of old Paris to where Notre-Dame squats in the dusk.
> . . . sometimes, if the day was bright, I would buy a liter of wine and a piece of bread and some sausage and sit in the sun and read one of the books I had bought and watch the fishing. . . . With the fishermen and the life on the river, the beautiful barges with their own life on board . . . the plane trees and in some places the poplars, I could never be lonely along the river.

Anaïs Nin, an American writer born in France, lived on a houseboat on the Seine in the 1930s when she hung out with Henry Miller and at Whitman's bookshop when it was called Mistral. She describes the tramps along the Seine as 'comical, humorous, their delirious oratory . . . often ironic and witty'.

## 12 **Gertrude Stein on the quais** 5e

Stein also loved the Quai de Montebello. Before taking a stairway across from Notre Dame to descend to the *quai* of the river, you will see the bookstalls, which have old pictures, postcards, and books, and down-river the Petit-Pont (small bridge), the oldest river-crossing in the city. The Romans built a wooden bridge there at the end of their road from Orleans (now rue Saint-Jacques). The architect of Notre Dame, Bishop Maurice of Sully, had a stone bridge constructed in 1185 and allowed minstrels to cross toll-free. Eleven times this bridge has been destroyed by fire or flood.

Stein describes the Quai de Montebello, facing Notre Dame, in *Paris France* in 1940:

> The quays in Paris have never changed, that is to say they look different but the life that goes on there is always the same. It was only last year that I really got to know them. I had put my car in a garage below Notre Dame and every morning and every evening I went the length of the quays forward and back. I found that going down below near the water I could let my dogs loose because we crossed no streets and then I found the life there below was very pleasant, it had nothing whatever to do with the life of a city.

Hemingway remembered, 'I would walk along the quais when I finished work or when I was trying to think something out'. Henry Miller also loved to wander along the Seine at night, 'going mad with the beauty of it, the trees leaning to, the broken images in the water'.

## 13  Cathedral of Notre Dame                                    4e

The cathedral of Paris has been for more than seven centuries one of the masterpieces of art. From the square in front, ground zero, all the road distances in France are measured. The popularity of Victor Hugo's *The Hunchback of Notre Dame* (1831) led to significant restoration of the cathedral in the 1840s.

Numerous American writers have mentioned the Notre Dame in their fiction or poetry. Typical of the response is that of Sinclair Lewis in *Dodsworth*, where 'the whole cathedral seemed to expand' before his eyes, 'the work of human hands seemed to tower larger than the sky'. Where Lewis sees French 'strength and endurance and wisdom' in Notre Dame, William Faulkner was amused by the pagan images.

**William Faulkner**, who was in Paris for nearly five months (see **map B**) in 1925, describes the 'grand' cathedral

> covered with cardinals mitred like Assyrian kings, and knights leaning on long swords, and saints and angels, and beautiful naked Greek

Hemingway 'stood on the crowded back platform' of a bus as it
'lurched along . . . passed Notre Dame grey and dripping in the rain'.

figures that have no religious significance whatever, and gargoyles — creatures with heads of goats and dogs, and claws and wings on men's bodies, all staring down in a jeering sardonic mirth.

If the external carving fascinated Faulkner, it was the romantic effect of the cathedral at twilight that captured the poetic eye of **E. E. Cummings** (see **map A**) in his volume, *Is 5*, written in Paris:

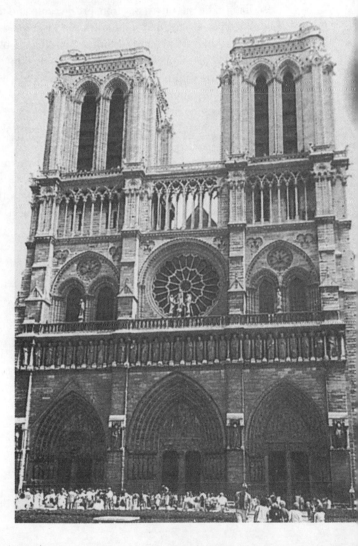

Notre Dame Cathedral, described by Hemingway and dozens of other American writers, as it looks today.

Paris; this April sunset completely utters
utters serenely silently a cathedral

before whose upward lean magnificent face
the streets turn young with rain.

This spring vision contrasts to his earlier mention in *The Enormous Room*, when just before Christmas in 1917 he walked past the cathedral without describing it: he was on his way from prison camp and the chill went through his mittens as he headed for the train and home.

As with other artistic and historical monuments of Paris, Hemingway occasionally mentions Notre Dame in his fiction and nonfiction. He observed Paris with a cinematic eye, documented its sharp scenes and captured living moments. The following scene, one of a group of six 'true sentences' he wrote in 1922 or 1923, illustrates the sharp eye witness of Hemingway and is closer to the spirit of Cummings than Faulkner:

I have stood on the crowded back platform of a seven o'clock Batignolles bus as it lurched along the wet damp street while men going home to supper never looked up from their newspapers as we passed Notre Dame grey and dripping in the rain.

Walk D begins on the smaller island behind the Cathedral and across the bridge. If you start the next walk now, begin with Site No. 3 and then find No. 1.

# 5

# HEMINGWAY'S FIRST HOME: CARDINAL-LEMOINE AND RUE MOUFFETARD

I live on the Ile St. Louis, in the Seine, a beautifully old seedy part
of Paris that I love — I spend my spare time writing and sketching
up and down the river.

John Dos Passos, in a little *pâtisserie* on the Ile Saint-Louis

In the 5th arrondissement (5e), east of the Boul' Mich', Ernest and Hadley Hemingway made their first home in Paris. They moved into an apartment near the top of the Montagne Saint-Geneviève (once inhabited by the Romans), in rue du Cardinal-Lemoine. Across the Place de la Contrescarpe was 'the narrow crowded world of the rue Mouffetard', as Hemingway's Harry remembers it in 'The Snows of Kilimanjaro': 'There was never another part of Paris that he loved like that'.

Hemingway was at his most intense and impressionable during this first year in Paris. He rented a room around the corner in rue Descartes in which to write. When he reached an impasse in his writing, he would plunge down the stairs of his working studio and into the narrow cobblestoned streets to absorb the impressions of this old quarter. He was particularly attentive to the workers and the drunks, the smell of food, and the movement of the Seine. He enjoyed crossing the bridges of Paris. For a visual writer, to whom place and detail are vital, the sights and sounds of this first neighbourhood were the background of his artistic development and the subject matter for short story and memoir. In both 'The Snows of Kilimanjaro' and *A Moveable Feast*, the protagonist/narrator is a man at the end of his life, his talent on the wane, who is looking back to the vital days of creative development. These are the streets and buildings that were the stage and impetus for his creative development.

The Latin Quarter is the home of the University of Paris, founded in 1215 and separated into 13 autonomous universities in 1970; the massive

## D Hemingway's First Home: Cardinal-Lemoine and rue Mouffetard

1 Au Rendez-vous des Mariniers
2 Three Mountains Press and *Transatlantic Review*
3 Harry and Caresse Crosby
4 Bridges (Sully and La Tournelle)
5 John Dos Passos
6 Rue du Cardinal-Lemoine
7 Hemingway's first home
8 Hemingway's studio
9 André Chamson
10 Café des Amateurs
11 Place de la Contrescarpe
12 Rue Mouffetard
13 Val-de-Grâce Church

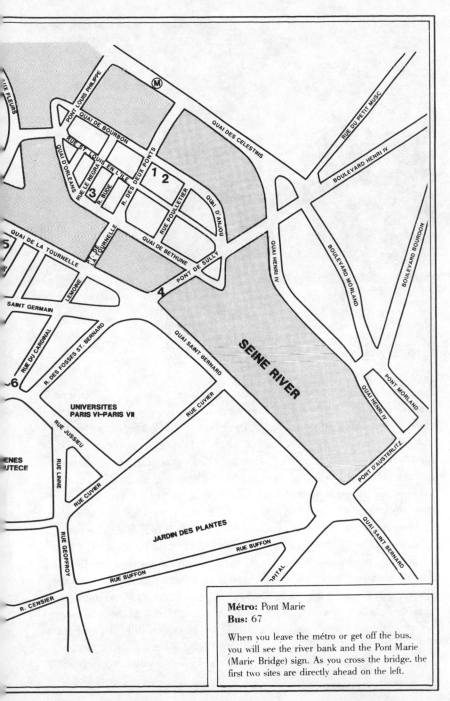

**Métro:** Pont Marie
**Bus:** 67

When you leave the métro or get off the bus, you will see the river bank and the Pont Marie (Marie Bridge) sign. As you cross the bridge, the first two sites are directly ahead on the left.

'At the head of the Ile de la Cité below the Pont Neuf . . . there was a small park at the water's edge with fine chestnut trees, huge and spreading, and in the currents and back waters that the Seine made flowing past, there were excellent places to fish.'
*A Moveable Feast*

Panthéon, burial place for Voltaire, Rousseau, Hugo, and others; Saint-Etienne-du-Mont church, where Pascal and Racine are buried; and the crowded old neighbourhood of the Place de la Contrescarpe. To the east lies the Jardin des Plantes, to the southwest the Val-de-Grâce Church. For Hemingway this region was characterized particularly by its narrow cobblestone streets and the working-class shops and stalls. Most of the cobblestone streets have recently been resurfaced and it is no longer the working-class neighbourhood it was in 1922. Yet enough remains to pique the imagination of those who read the opening pages of *A Moveable Feast*.

Before visiting the Place de la Contrescarpe region of Hemingway's first Paris home, begin with a visit to the quiet island called Ile Saint-Louis, where you can drop into one of the many tea rooms or picnic and meditate on the benches along the *quai*. Hemingway loved the *quais* and the river, patronized little cafés here, and was a regular in 1923 at the offices of two important expatriate presses on the Quai d'Anjou: Bill Bird's Three Mountains Press publishing company and Ford's *Transatlantic Review*.

John Dos Passos, before he had published any novels, lived between

1918 and 1921 in three different apartments located in the territory covered by this chapter. The first one was located on the Ile Saint-Louis, where he lived in July 1918, not long after having met Hemingway briefly in Italy. Dos Passos describes this 'beautifully old seedy part of Paris'. While drinking cold chocolate in a little *pâtisserie* here he wrote home to a friend, 'I spend my spare time writing and sketching up and down the river . . . and wander about and go to little restaurants and outlandish little cafes'.

Whether you visit one or all of the sites on the island — and there is nothing to see but the façades of the original buildings — you should walk the *quais* and look inside any historical buildings to which the doors are open. Capture a sense of the comfort and quiet of this island.

**1  Au Rendez-vous des Mariniers:** 33 Quai d'Anjou          4e

Paris was a feast for the eyes as well as the stomach. This quiet, tree-lined island and this small family restaurant drew two American writers who would become longtime friends: Hemingway and Dos Passos. They skied, fished, and ate together in numerous places from Europe to Florida. In fact, John Dos Passos would later meet his wife, Katy, a childhood friend of Ernest Hemingway, at the latter's home in Key West.

Near Pont-Marie was Madame Lecomte's hotel and restaurant, called Au Rendez-vous des Mariniers, which Hemingway uses in *The Sun Also Rises*. Bill and Jake take a taxi to Ile Saint-Louis.

> We ate dinner at Madame Lecomte's restaurant on the far side of the island. It was crowded with Americans and we had to stand up and wait for a place. Someone had put it in the American Women's Club list as a quaint restaurant on the Paris quais as yet untouched by Americans, so we had to wait forty-five minutes for a table. Bill had eaten at the restaurant in 1918, and right after the armistice, and Madame Lecomte made a great fuss over seeing him.
>
> 'Doesn't get us a table, though,' Bill said. 'Grand woman, though.'
>
> We had a good meal, a roast chicken, new green beans, mashed potatoes, a salad, and some apple-pie and cheese.
>
> 'You've got the world here all right,' Bill said to Madame Lecomte. She raised her hand. 'Oh, my God!'
>
> 'You'll be rich.'
>
> 'I hope so.'
>
> After coffee and a *fine* we got the bill, chalked up the same as

ever on a slate, that was doubtless one of the 'quaint' features, paid it, shook hands, and went out.

'You never come here any more, Monsieur Barnes,' Madame Lecomte said.

'Too many compatriots.'

Earlier the Lecomte hotel and restaurant had been a haven for John Dos Passos in 1918, when he was on his way home from the war in Italy. He stayed in Paris hoping, unsuccessfully, to straighten out a charge of disloyalty against him with the Red Cross. During this time Dos Passos, who spoke French very well, became an extension of the family Lecomte. While waiting, he had plenty of time to begin the planning and writing of what would later become *Three Soldiers* and *One Man's Initiation: 1917*. Big Bertha was still dropping bombs on the city as he left for home. He returned in the spring of 1920 hoping to sell his completed *Three Soldiers* manuscript to a British publisher. He headed his letters 'en face du Pont Marie comme autre fois', and referred to his novel as 'the second great American novel' or 'the triune doughboy'. George H. Duran finally accepted it after 13 publishers rejected it.

A dining guide written by an American in the decade when Hemingway and Dos Passos patronized Madame Lecomte's restaurant describes it as a 'queer little place, very French', with zinc bar, marble-topped tables, and paper napkins.

Even today this part of Paris gives you a sense of the more quiet atmosphere of the 1920s and illustrates why Hemingway loved the river and bridges of Paris. Sit on the embankment opposite No. 29.

## 2 Three Mountains Press office/Transatlantic Review editorial office: 29 Quai d'Anjou                                         4e

### Three Mountains Press office

In the cellar or ground floor of No. 29 (the medieval façade has been renovated) were two of the important publishers of the Modernist period.

William Bird, a journalist who had founded the Consolidated Press Association in 1919 and had become its European manager in 1920, founded the Three Mountains Press. Bird's press was one of the finest hand presses, built in the seventeenth century. Hemingway met Bird in the spring of 1922 at the Genoa Economic Conference, which both

William (Bill) Bird, friend and publisher of Hemingway's *in our time*, which he hand set on his Three Mountains Press in 1924 at 29 Quai d'Anjou.

journalists were covering. A year later, Bird suggested that Hemingway write a dozen more miniature stories or sketches like the ones he had published in the Spring 1923 Exile's Number of the *Little Review*. Henry Strater, a friend of Hemingway, did a woodcut portrait for a frontispiece. Before he and Hadley returned to Toronto in August 1923, Hemingway completed his writing and submitted the manuscript to Bird.

In 1924 Bird published Hemingway's *in our time* (the title printed without capitalization) in this one-time wine-vault on the banks of the Seine. This volume enabled Hemingway to win his first American contract, with Boni and Liveright, who insisted that 'Up in Michigan' could not be included. Bird also published books by Ford Madox Ford, William Carlos Williams, Robert McAlmon, and Ezra Pound (who served for a while as his editor). This was also the *Transatlantic Review* office.

## Transatlantic Review editorial office

Beginning late in 1923, William Bird shared his press office with Ford Madox Ford's magazine, which occupied the gallery.

The *transatlantic review* (the title printed without capitalization), published between January and December 1924, presenting works by Pound, Conrad, Ford, Cummings, Stein (*The Making of Americans*), Joyce, Tristan Tzara, William Carlos Williams, Dos Passos, Djuna Barnes, and Hemingway. Ford was particularly keen about American writers from the

Midwest, though he did not feel that his writers always treated him with enough respect: 'I really exist as a sort of half-way house between nonpublishable youth and real money', Ford told Stein, 'a sort of green baize door that every one kicks both on entering and on leaving'.

Ford gave weekly parties that spilled out of their cramped headquarters. (Eventually he had to move the parties to a large apartment he shared with Stella Bowen in Boulevard Arago, then to a dance hall up the hill in rue du Cardinal-Lemoine, below Hemingway's first apartment.) Hemingway usually appeared at Ford's Thursday teas wearing worn tennis shoes and a patched jacket. Ford describes the scene as follows:

> I do not think that there would ever have been an artistic atmosphere younger or more pleasurable or more cordial than that which surrounded the *Review* offices and the Thursday teas. . . . On most Thursdays Mr Hemingway shadow boxed at Mr Bird's press, at the files of unsold reviews, and at my nose, shot tree-leopards that twined through the rails of the editorial galley and told magnificent tales of the boundless prairies of his birth. . . . Mr Hemingway soon became my assistant editor.

'Ford asked me to read MSS for him', wrote Hemingway, 'and I used to go down there and take a batch of them out on the Quai and read them'. (Note the stairway that Hemingway took down to the riverbank.) When Ford went to the United States to raise money (unsuccessfully) for the review, Hemingway edited the July and August 1924 numbers. It was Hemingway who eventually found a friend to finance publication to the end of the year.

Ford claims that he 'did not read more than six words' of Hemingway before he 'decided to publish everything that he sent me'. The appearance of 'Indian Camp' in the April 1924 issue brought Hemingway's name to the attention of the Paris expatriate world.

In this office Hemingway met Harold Loeb, a Princeton graduate and editor of *Broom*. The two men spent many afternoons of 1924 playing tennis together on the courts in Boulevard Arago. Loeb remembers that Hemingway did not run up to the net because of his bad leg, injured by shrapnel. (Hadley says that both Loeb and she played better tennis than Hemingway.) Loeb introduced Hemingway to Leon Fleischman of Boni and Liveright, who later published *In Our Time* (now capitalized) in the United States. In his memoirs, *The Way it Was*, Harold Loeb says he met Hemingway here:

> It was there that I met Ernest Hemingway, who was helping Ford get out the review. He had a shy, disarming smile and did not seem interested in the other guests; he wore sneakers, my favorite footgear, and a patched jacket. I thought never before had I encountered an American so unaffected by living in Paris.

Hemingway repaid the friendship with a satire of Loeb as Robert Cohn in *The Sun Also Rises* (1926).

Next-door at No. 27 was the famous literary salon of the Marquise de Lambert. Continue along the *quai* to circle the island or to cut through rue Poulletier to the Quai de Béthune. If you circle around the tip of the island, note the Hôtel de Lauzun (enter No. 17), now used for official city guests, at various times the home of Théophile Gautier, Baudelaire, Rilke, Sickert, and Wagner. Note the gilded balconies and water spouts. If you cut through on rue Poulletier, note the clock on the church belltower in rue Saint-Louis-en-l'Ile.

As you stand on the Quai de Béthune (Helena Rubenstein lived at No. 24) you will see Sully Bridge on the left (where you will proceed up the hill of Saint-Geneviève to Hemingway's home) and Tournelle Bridge (the statue of Saint-Geneviève was built in 1928) to the right. If you choose to take a 15-minute detour to the Dos Passos site (No. 5), read No. 4 now while you are close to Pont de Sully.

**3  Harry and Caresse Crosby: 12 Quai d'Orléans**               4e

The Crosbys lived in the summer of 1923 at the corner of Quai d'Orléans and rue Budé (look for the blue metal balcony) to the right as you face the water. They had a canoe tied to the riverbank (beneath the metal stairway) and sometimes Harry would paddle the canoe to the Tuileries and walk to work at the bank. Before coming to Paris, he had worked in the home bank of his family (J. P. Morgan). The wealthy Crosbys were not in Hemingway's circle when they lived here in 1923: Crosby owned racehorses, Hemingway just bet on them. But by 1927, when Hemingway had fame and a new socially conscious wife, Pauline, they partied and travelled together: to the bullfights in Pamplona in 1927, to the Riviera, to the races at Auteuil in 1928. The Crosbys, who then lived in the rue de Lille, were a part of the literary world by virtue of their Black Sun Press, established in 1927. (Harry Crosby committed suicide in 1929.)

According to Crosby's biographer, Crosby and Hemingway shared several things:

> Mutual admiration, an affection for French customs and places, a religion based on literary principles, suicide, and a special fondness for the words of Feeble wasted upon Falstaff in *Henry the Fourth: Part Two:* 'By my troth I care not, a man can die but once, we owe God a death. . . . An't be my destiny.

The homes on the *quais* of Ile Saint-Louis, now some of the most costly land in Paris, have been renovated to a condition of earlier days, when many wealthy expatriates lived here — such as Nancy Cunard, who lived at 2 rue Le Regattier just a few steps beyond the Crosbys. Hemingway frequently stopped at Cunard's apartment after working on the *Transatlantic Review*.

In *The Sun Also Rises*, Jake and Bill walk along under the trees that line this *quai* after eating at Madame Lecomte's restaurant.

## 4 Bridges (Sully and La Tournelle) 4e

'It is always pleasant crossing bridges in Paris', observes Jake in *The Sun Also Rises*. Both these bridges took him from the island up the hill to his home: Pont-de-Sully, named after Henry IV's minister when it was built in 1874–6, and Pont-de-la-Tournelle, which dates from 1369. Because La Tournelle was destroyed and rebuilt between 1923 and 1928, during the time that Hemingway was in Paris, he describes the following walk of Jake Barnes and Bill Gorton as traversing the temporary wooden bridge built nearby and used during that construction:

> We walked on and circled the island. The river was dark and a bateau mouche went by, all bright with lights, going fast and quiet up and out of sight under the bridge. Down the river was Notre-Dame squatting against the night sky. We crossed to the left bank of the Seine by the wooden footbridge from the Quai de Béthune, and stopped on the bridge and looked down the river at Notre-Dame. Standing on the bridge the island looked dark, the houses were high against the sky, and the trees were shadows.

Sully bridge (Pont-de-Sully) taken from Quai de Béthune. Ile Saint-
Louis. One of the routes to Hemingway's home in rue Cardinal-
Lemoine.

'It's pretty grand,' Bill said. 'God I love to get back.'

We leaned on the wooden rail of the bridge and looked up the
river to the lights of the big bridges. Below the water was smooth
and black. It made no sound against the piles of the bridge. A man
and a girl passed us, they were walking with their arms around each
other.

We crossed the bridge and walked up the Rue du Cardinal
Lemoine. It was steep walking.

Whichever bridge you take, pause midstream for a look up and
down the river. If you take the Sully bridge, on the other side turn
right a few yards before crossing the street and climbing the hill. Cross
both Quai de la Tournelle and Boulevard Saint-Germain, keeping to your
left the modernistic Institute of the Arab World and the university — where
Hemingway saw the Halle aux Vins, wine distribution centre for Paris.
As you walk up rue des Fossés-Saint-Bernard you will enter rue du
Cardinal-Lemoine (No. 6), where three blocks up is the first Hemingway
home (No. 7).

## 5 John Dos Passos: 45 Quai de la Tournelle                5e

One door west of the rue de Pontoise is No. 45, next-door to the Social Service (Welfare) Museum, where John Dos Passos lived in the springs of 1919 and 1921, before Hemingway's arrival in Paris. Just discharged from the American Ambulance Corps in 1919, he was registered as a candidate for a doctorate at the University of Paris and 'crazy' with spring fever — 'I feel like . . . an incarnation of Dionysus' — and the spell of Paris — 'at any moment I expect the roof of the house to open like the corolla of a flower, or the gutters of the Quai de la Tournelle to run . . . amethysts'.

He began *Three Soldiers* (1921) here and, after climbing in the Pyrenees with his friend E. E. Cummings, returned to finish *Rosinante to the Road Again* (1922). His wartime experiences in France were published in *One Man's Initiation: 1917* (1920).

Dos Passos would later become a good friend of Hemingway when in the summer of 1924 the men partied together in Paris. Hemingway suggested to Ford that he publish Dos Passos. 'July', an early sketch from *Manhattan Transfer*, appeared that summer in the *Transatlantic Review*.

The best views of Notre Dame are from this *quai*. Walk up rue de Pontoise, where Hemingway says he earned 10 francs sparring in a gym (probably at No.6 on the right) with professional heavyweights in 1924. This sparring story may have been invented to exaggerate his 'poverty'. In his memoirs he refers to a bathhouse (probably the Latin Quarter pool on the left):

> I thought of bathtubs and showers and toilets that flushed as things that inferior people to us had or that you enjoyed when you made trips, which we often made. There was always the public bathhouse down at the foot of the street by the river.

At the end of rue Pontoise, turn left to join rue du Cardinal-Lemoine at the stop light.

## 6 Rue du Cardinal-Lemoine                6e

Although this is the steepest climb up the hill to Hemingway's first home, it was the shortest route from his visits with Bird. In *The Sun Also Rises*, Jake and Bill walk from the Ile Saint-Louis up rue du Cardinal-Lemoine. Past rue Monge the street is virtually unchanged. At rue Clovis you get a view to the right of the Panthéon. Before the street narrows into Place de la Contrescarpe, you pass No. 71 on the left. At the end of this long drive at No. 71 lived Valéry Larbaud, the French polyglot translator and critic, and friend of Beach and Monnier. Larbaud lent his flat to the James Joyce family from June to October 1921, just two months before Hemingway arrived in Paris. A few more steps up the street, on the right (beside the discothèque), is the location where Hadley and Ernest Hemingway made their first home in Paris.

**7  Hemingway's first home:** 74 rue du Cardinal-Lemoine        5e

From the Hôtel Jacob et d'Angleterre, Hemingway moved into this fourth-floor walk-up in an old, working-class district. The building is on a street (once cobblestoned) that climbs the hill overlooking Pont Sully and just

Hemingway's first apartment was on the fourth floor at 74 rue du Cardinal-Lemoine. As then, there is a dance hall to the left.

a few steps before the Place de la Contrescarpe. He and Hadley found it with the help of Lewis Galantière and rented it on 9 January 1922. It was a two-room flat without hot water or toilet 'except an antiseptic container, not uncomfortable to anyone who was used to a Michigan outhouse', recalled Hemingway in his memoir. 'The steep winding staircase had a niche on each flight for a step-on-two-pedals toilet', recalled Hadley, who spent long hours and weeks in their apartment while he travelled for the *Toronto Star* or worked at a studio around the corner. Rent control laws kept Paris rents very cheap (and plumbing antiquated), and they could have lived in a better district. With Ernest's journalism and Hadley's trust fund and an inheritance from her uncle, they had about $5000 income that first year, after investing the inheritance. But he valued travel, vacations, and sporting events more highly than living quarters, and he had inherited his father's parsimony.

In March 1922, Stein and Toklas visited the apartment, crowded with heavy furniture; Stein, settling herself on the mahogany bed to read everything Ernest had written, disapproved of the sexual frankness of his short story 'Up in Michigan'. She liked his 'direct, Kiplingesque' poetry, but not his attempt at a first novel, which was too descriptive. 'Begin over again and concentrate', she suggested.

On the ground-floor next-door was a *bal musette* (popular dance hall) which occasionally awakened them in the night. It was called Bal du Printemps in the 1920s, but is now Le Rayon Vert discothèque. In *A Moveable Feast*, after Ford Madox Ford invites the Hemingways to a party at this *bal musette*, Hemingway informs him that he knows the place and 'the man who owns it had a taxi and when I had to get to a plane he'd taken me out to the field'. (According to Michael Reynolds, Hemingway flew only once.) *In the Sun Also Rises* Jake Barnes and Georgette Hobin are invited to visit a *bal musette* in this region by a man named Braddocks, who is based on Ford:

> When we arrived it was quite empty, except for a policeman sitting near the door, the wife of the proprietor back of the zinc bar, and the proprietor himself. The daughter of the house came downstairs as we went in. There were long benches, and tables ran across the room, and at the far end a dancing-floor.
>
> 'I wish people would come earlier,' Braddocks said. The daughter came up and wanted to know what we would drink. The proprietor got up on a high stool beside the dancing-floor and began to play

the accordion. He had a string of bells around one of his ankles and beat time with his foot as he played. Everyone danced. It was hot and we came off the floor perspiring.

'My God', Georgette said. 'What a box to sweat in!'

Walk a few steps back around the corner into rue Thouin. Hemingway's studio is to the right in rue Descartes, and rue Mouffetard is to the left. In 'The Snows of Kilimanjaro', his alter ego Harry recalls this neighbourhood:

> There was never another part of Paris that he loved like that, the sprawling trees, the old white plastered houses painted brown below, the long green of the autobus in that round square, the purple flower dye upon the paving, the sudden drop down the hill of the rue Cardinal Lemoine to the river, and the other way the narrow crowded world of the rue Mouffetard.

## 8  Hemingway's studio: 39 rue Descartes                     5e

For a brief time in 1922, Hemingway rented an attic room in this small hotel (now an apartment building), where poet Paul Verlaine had died 25 years before. For 60 francs a month he used a top-floor room as a studio for writing (while he lived around the corner in rue du Cardinal-Lemoine).

> The fireplace drew well in the room and it was warm and pleasant to work. I brought mandarines and roasted chestnuts to the room in paper packets and peeled and ate the small tangerine-like oranges and threw their skins and spat their seeds in the fire . . . and roasted chestnuts when I was hungry . . . I would stand and look out over the roofs of Paris and think, 'Do not worry. You have always written before and you will write now. All you have to do is write one true sentence' . . .
>
> It was wonderful to walk down the long flights of stairs knowing that I'd had good luck working. I always worked until I had something done and I always stopped when I knew what was going to happen next. That way I could be sure of going on the next day.

In 'The Snows of Kilimanjaro', he says he could see the roofs and chimney

The studio at 39 rue Descartes, where Hemingway wrote during part of 1922: 'the climb up to the top floor of the hotel where I worked, in a room that looked across all the roofs and the chimneys of the high hill of the quarter, was a pleasure'.

pots and all the hills of Paris from this room. In this cheap room with a rich view, he wrote short stories of his boyhood Michigan.

When Hemingway lived here, the neighbourhood was noisy, beggars asked for alms, and drunks slept in the bistro doorways. Since the 1950s these *clochards* (vagrants) have had to make room for the students. Though a shirtsleeve working-class neighbourhood, this quarter was rich in historical and literary associations, with the Panthéon and the remains of the Roman amphitheatre (Les Arènes de Lutèce) nearby.

Earlier, John Dos Passos lived briefly somewhere on this street. It was 1917 and he was between ambulance-driving assignments for Norton-Harjes and the Red Cross (in Italy). In the spring of 1919 he found a place down the hill from here where he reworked 'Seven Times Round the Walls of Jericho' at his typewriter 'from morning till night with interval for food — delicious sizzly Paris food and concerts'.

At No. 25 in a little bar-room, A Dauguet's place, the famous four sergeants of La Rochelle plotted against Napoleon.

When you turn toward the Place de la Contrescarpe (left as you leave Maison de Verlaine), you will cross rue Thouin. The building where Chamson lived is gone.

## 9 André Chamson: 17 rue Thouin                    5e

André and Lucie Chamson were friends of Sylvia Beach, who introduced them to the Hemingways. She also introduced them to Fitzgerald and King Vidor (the American film director) in the hope of having Vidor use Chamson's *Les Hommes de la Route* for a movie. Though the movie deal fell through, Fitzgerald and Chamson became good friends.

Fitzgerald visited the Chamsons in their humble, sixth-floor apartment with a view of the Panthéon. (The original building has been replaced by an ugly brick building at No. 15, next to the pretty little park. Diderot had lived on the other side of the park.) Chamson later recalled Fitzgerald's arrival in the May sunlight: 'He came into my life with that smile and probably because of the sunlight coming through the stairway window . . . as though in a halo of light'. Without a language in common or a common background, the men in 'a sort of lightning stroke', became good friends. Both Chamsons had distinguished educations. Though a devoted and respected writer, Chamson was then earning his income as a reporter covering the Chamber of Deputies. He later wrote the introduction to the French translation of *The Great Gatsby*.

Return back down the rue Thouin and turn right at No. 1 rue Mouffetard.

## 10 Café des Amateurs: Place de la Contrescarpe         5e

During Hemingway's first year in Paris, this café ('around the corner' from his home are the only directions we have) was crowded with drunks and full of smells. The café was 'a sad, evilly run café', and he called it 'the cesspool of the rue Mouffetard' in the poetic opening pages of *A Moveable Feast*: 'No [horse-drawn tank wagons] emptied the Café des Amateurs [cesspool] though, and its yellowed poster stating the terms and penalties of the law against public drunkenness was as flyblown and disregarded as its clients were constant and ill-smelling'.

Today, with the influx of more students and tourists, the cafés are certainly more hospitable, though hardly first class. The Amateurs, if Hemingway remembered the name correctly, was probably where La Chope is located today, on the north side of the Place.

In *The Sun Also Rises*, Jake and Bill stop here after their dinner at Madame Lecomte's restaurant on the Ile Saint-Louis:

It was steep walking, and we went all the way up to the Place

Contrescarpe. The arc-light shone through the leaves of the trees in the square, and underneath the trees was an S bus ready to start. Music came out of the door of the Nègre Joyeux. Through the window of the Café Aux Amateurs I saw the long zinc bar. Outside on the terrace working people were drinking. In the open kitchen of the Amateurs a girl was cooking potato chips in oil. There was an iron pot of stew. The girl ladled some onto a plate for an old man who stood holding a bottle of red wine in one hand.

## 11  Place de la Contrescarpe                                      5e

This tiny village square is central to the early months of the Hemingways' life in Paris. The medieval name (escarpment: steep face or slope) reminds one that it is on the site of the moat that once surrounded Paris. One of the gates of Phillip Augustus' wall stood nearby. This square (at the corner of rue Blainville) once contained the Cabaret de la Pomme de Pin (pine cone) mentioned by Rabelais and Ronsard and where the Pléiade literary society began in 1549 (founded by Pierre Ronsard, Joachim Du Bellay and Jean Baif).

Have a coffee on the terrace of one of the cafés. The 5½ francs are worth the view of village life. Hemingway loved the bustle of this quarter, but he also enjoyed the quiet *quais* of Ile Saint-Louis.

In 'The Snows of Kilimanjaro', Hemingway's Harry recalls the characters and sights of the Place de la Contrescarpe with nostalgia:

Around that Place there were two kinds; the drunkards and the sportifs. The drunkards killed their poverty that way; the sportifs took it out in exercise. They were the descendants of the Communards and it was no struggle for them to know their politics. They knew who had shot their fathers, their relatives, their brothers, and their friends when the Versailles troops came in and took the town after the Commune and executed any one they could catch with calloused hands, or who wore a cap, or carried any other sign he was a working man.

Despite the presence of tourists at each terrace, the *clochards* still rest against the trees of the square, sharing a litre among themselves. William Wiser

(*The Crazy Years*) notes their resemblance to Vladimir and Estragon in *Waiting for Godot* by Samuel Beckett. A little more than five years after Hemingway's residence in this quarter, Beckett lived west of rue Mouffetard in rue d'Ulm.

Diagonally across the square from rue du Cardinal-Lemoine and Hemingway's home is rue Mouffetard. Rue du Pot-de-Fer is the first street down the hill, though you may wish to detour to the bottom of rue Mouffetard.

## 12  Rue Mouffetard                                                      5e

One of the most picturesque streets in Paris, the rue Mouffetard is a narrow street that plunges down to the broad rue Censier. In the mornings four days a week (especially Saturday), on the lowest and steepest section of this ancient road to Italy, is the teeming open-air market (le Mouff') with its high piles of vegetables, dozens of kinds of shellfish, hanging rabbits, chickens, and quail. Here is where Hemingway bought the mandarin oranges and chestnuts that he nibbled while he wrote short stories.

Sections of the street are considerably changed since the 1930s when two streets were driven through rue Mouffetard (at which time excavators discovered Louis XIV gold pieces). Although the Greek restaurants and pizzerias now alternate with market stalls, a renaissance of boutiques and remodelled apartments is creeping into rue Mouffetard.

To follow Hemingway's steps from rue Mouffetard to the cafés of Montparnasse and the quarter in which he next lived, angle toward the intersection of the Boulevards Port-Royal and Montparnasse, by staying north of Val-de-Grâce Church. In *The Sun Also Rises*, Bill and Jake turn right off rue Mouffetard (at the curved corner building) into rue du Pot-de-Fer — made famous in George Orwell's *Down and Out in Paris and London*. They 'follow it along' five connecting streets: rue de Pot-de-Fer becomes rue Rataud, right on rue Erasme; at the entrance to Ecole Normale Supérieure, rue Louis Thuillier and rue des Ursulines will take you to rue Saint-Jacques. Bill and Jake entered rue Saint-Jacques 'and then walked south, past Val-de-Grâce, set back behind the courtyard and the iron fence'.

Turn left into the rue Saint-Jacques (Saint James), the ancient route of pilgrims toward Spain to Santiago de Compostela. Back in the centuries when Latin was the language of the quarter, this was its main street.

## 13 Val-de-Grâce: 277 bis rue Saint-Jacques 5e

Alone among the abbeys of Paris, this domed church ('The Valley of Grace')
has kept its seventeenth-century building intact. The Convent of the
Carmelites and a hospital for wounded soldiers are housed here.

Val-de-Grâce church on rue Saint-Jacques. In *The Sun Also Rises*, Jake
and Bill 'walked south, past Val-de-Grâce, set back behind the
courtyard and the iron fence'.

When he walked from rue Mouffetard, Hemingway often passed here on his way to Montparnasse. In *The Sun Also Rises*, he inaccurately describes the curved medieval rue Saint-Jacques as a 'rigid north and south' street. Within a few yards of this abbey had lived Pasteur, Lamennais, La Fontaine, and George Sand. Rue Saint-Jacques crosses Boulevard du Port-Royal, which will take you (right) to Closerie de Lilas and the beginning of **map E**.

Just across the Boulevard du Port-Royal — somewhere in rue de la Santé — lived Hemingway's friend Morley Callaghan, a Canadian writer, in 1929. They had known each other in Toronto at the *Star*. Morley and Loretto lived above a grocery store near La Santé prison. Nearby was A la Bonne Santé, a bistro where the Harry Crosbys, Kay Boyle, and Robert McAlmon awaited the release of Hart Crane from prison in the summer of 1929. Crane had been arrested after a fight at the Café Sélect, and Crosby had paid the fine. Two blocks east at 147 rue Broca lived another Canadian writer named John Glassco (*Memoirs of Montparnasse*) in 1928. Glassco was a friend of McAlmon, not of Hemingway.

In his memoirs of *That Summer in Paris*, subtitled 'memories of tangled friendships with Hemingway, Fitzgerald, and some others', Callaghan writes about the summer of 1929. He boxed with Hemingway and frequented the Montparnasse cafés, calling this quarter 'a very small, backbiting, gossipy little neighbourhood'. The Callaghans did not like Hemingway's second wife, Pauline, who disapproved of 'café sitting'.

You can end this walk and begin walk E with some café sitting on the terrace of the Closerie des Lilas, a Hemingway favourite, near the junction of the Boulevard du Port-Royal, Boulevard du Montparnasse and Boulevard Saint-Michel.

# 6

# MONTPARNASSE:
# THE EXPATRIATES

They went back to their own countries — the Americans were the
worst — and wrote righteous and moralizing articles and editorials
on expatriate life on the continent. Such articles always disgust me,
because knowing London and her pubs, New York and her speak-
easies, as well as Paris, I see no use in the lousy pretence that people
who drink don't drink elsewhere than in Paris.

Robert McAlmon, between the Dôme and the Rotonde

Ernest and Hadley Hemingway moved from the Place de la Contrescarpe
to the heart of expatriate Paris when they returned from Toronto with
their baby boy in 1924. This quarter was once called Mont Parnassus;
the 'hill', a mound of quarry rubble that students named after the dwelling
place of the Greek muses, was razed in the eighteenth century. In the
nineteenth century the polka and can-can were introduced in the cafés
and cabarets here on the outskirts of Paris. By the turn of the twentieth
century, it was a bohemian centre.

In the triangle of land between the Observatory, the Luxembourg
Gardens, and the Montparnasse station — and crossed by the Boulevard
du Montparnasse — lie the famous cafés of the 1920s. Here the summer
sun shone on the green Pernod in glasses on marble tables, and one could
spy the red-bearded Pound or the muscular Hemingway sitting in
conversation with friends. 'Every afternoon the people one knows can be
found at the café', wrote Hemingway in one of his poems.

Almost every French artist and writer — as well as their visiting
colleagues — served an apprenticeship in one Paris café or another. In
the *New York Times Book Review*, Anatole Broyard notes that in an
open-air café, a writer gets a sense of the world and who his audience
is; he can 'clear his head, lose the mothball smell of literature'. Hemingway
was one of the well-known café habitués. 'Gertrude Stein shunned cafés',
Broyard observes with amusement, 'and that may be the trouble with her

work; nobody in a café, even for free drinks, would have sat still for all those repetitions'. Hemingway's compatriot Thomas Wolfe captures, in *Of Time and the River*, the colour, play of life, and intoxication of odours that are café life in Paris:

All these elements, together with that incomparable fusion of odours — at once corrupt and sensual, subtle and obscene — which exudes from the very texture of the Paris life — odours which it is impossible to define exactly but which seem in the dull wintry air to be compacted of the smells of costly perfumes, of wine, beer, brandy, and of the acrid and nostalgic fumes of French tobacco, of roasted chestnuts, black French coffee, mysterious liquors of a hundred brilliant and intoxicating colors, and the luxurious flesh of scented women.

Hemingway lived around the corner from the café called La Closerie des Lilas, near his literary friends Pound and Stein. He loved to write in the Closerie des Lilas, walk through the Luxembourg, or meet a friend at the Sélect. During his residency in this quarter he became involved with Ford's *Transatlantic Review* and Ernest Walsh's *This Quarter* magazine. He also wrote 'Indian Camp', 'Big Two-Hearted River', and nearly a dozen other short stories. During a skiing trip to Austria he wrote that he needed the stimulation of a 'big town' like Paris in order to write.

Immediately after the Pamplona festival in July 1925, Hemingway began writing *The Sun Also Rises*, based upon his experiences in the bars of Paris (he met Fitzgerald at the Dingo that year) and the bullring of Pamplona, Spain. Later that year Boni and Liveright published his short stories *In Our Time* (with capitalization). When Hemingway wrote *The Torrents of Spring*, a satire of Sherwood Anderson's *Dark Laughter*, Liveright refused to publish this attack on their best-selling author. Hemingway was then free to sign with Scribner's, Fitzgerald's publisher.

In the Montparnasse quarter, Hemingway expanded his literary associations and emerged as an established writer. Here he let his hair grow longer and his clothes grow scruffy. Here also he ended his first marriage. After he became romantically involved with Pauline Pfeiffer, he and Hadley moved into separate apartments in this quarter, until their agreement to divorce in 1926. The divorce was final in 1927. His marriage to Pauline eventually took him from Paris to Key West, Florida.

Because he lived the longest in this quarter, the centre of social life,

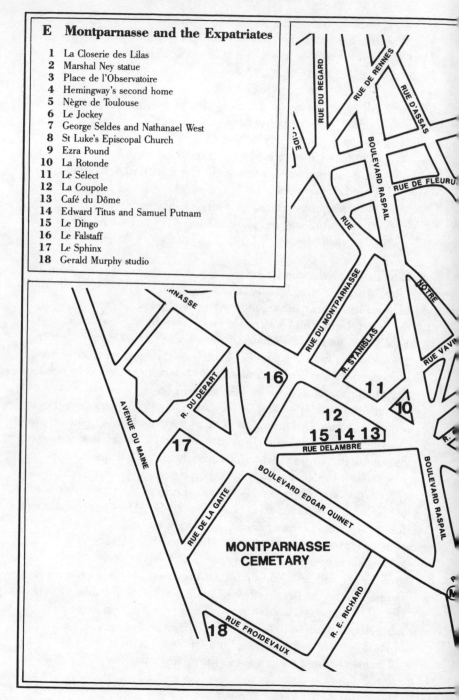

**E  Montparnasse and the Expatriates**

1  La Closerie des Lilas
2  Marshal Ney statue
3  Place de l'Observatoire
4  Hemingway's second home
5  Nègre de Toulouse
6  Le Jockey
7  George Seldes and Nathanael West
8  St Luke's Episcopal Church
9  Ezra Pound
10  La Rotonde
11  Le Sélect
12  La Coupole
13  Café du Dôme
14  Edward Titus and Samuel Putnam
15  Le Dingo
16  Le Falstaff
17  Le Sphinx
18  Gerald Murphy studio

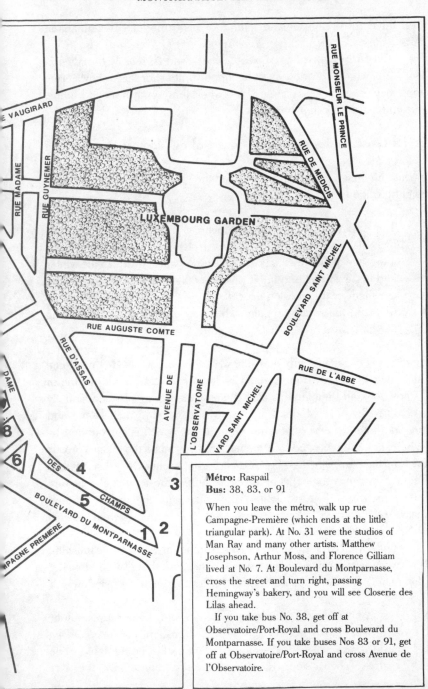

**Métro:** Raspail
**Bus:** 38, 83, or 91

When you leave the métro, walk up rue Campagne-Première (which ends at the little triangular park). At No. 31 were the studios of Man Ray and many other artists. Matthew Josephson, Arthur Moss, and Florence Gilliam lived at No. 7. At Boulevard du Montparnasse, cross the street and turn right, passing Hemingway's bakery, and you will see Closerie des Lilas ahead.

If you take bus No. 38, get off at Observatoire/Port-Royal and cross Boulevard du Montparnasse. If you take buses Nos 83 or 91, get off at Observatoire/Port-Royal and cross Avenue de l'Observatoire.

it provided subject matter and setting for his 'American Bohemians in Paris' (*Toronto Star Weekly*), *Torrents of Spring, The Sun Also Rises, The Green Hills of Africa, A Moveable Feast*, and *Islands in the Stream*. This walk, which provides too many opportunities for leisurely watering stops, begins at the Closerie des Lilas and Hemingway's second home, and ends at the Falstaff bar.

## 1  La Closerie des Lilas: 171 Boulevard du Montparnasse  6e

In his memoirs, Hemingway recalls the pleasure of his favourite neighbourhood café:

> The Closerie des Lilas was the nearest good café when we lived in the flat over the sawmill at 113 rue Notre-Dame-des-Champs, and it was one of the best cafés in Paris. It was warm inside in the winter and in the spring and fall it was fine outside with the table under the shade of the trees on the side where the statue of Marshal Ney was, and the square, regular tables under the big awnings along the boulevard.

Hemingway began his early-morning writing in this quiet café ('my home cafe') after his return from Canada in January 1924. While writing in his notebook and nursing his *café crème*, Hemingway was occasionally interrupted by Ford Madox Ford, who lived nearby. Most Dôme and Rotonde habitués never came up to the Lilas, which is surrounded by high bushes and protected by Marshal Ney. (Nowadays the bushes protect one from the sight of the ugly building across the Avenue de l'Observatoire.) Hemingway remembers that in the early 1920s 'most of the clients were elderly men in well worn clothes who came with their wives or their mistresses'. In the evenings Hemingway sat outside and watched the light change on the trees and on the buildings.

Hemingway met MacLeish here in the summer of 1924, while finishing 'Big Two-Hearted River', which he called the 'best thing I have done by a long shot'. He wrote the short story on a table near the window:

> I sat in a corner with the afternoon light coming in over my shoulder and wrote in the notebook. The waiter brought me a *café crème* and I drank half of it when it cooled and left it on the table while I wrote. When I stopped writing I did not want to leave the river

'My home café', Hemingway called Closerie des Lilas, where he began writing 'Big Two-Hearted River' and where he worked on the revision of *The Sun Also Rises*.

where I could see the trout in the pool.

On this terrace he also did some writing on the first complete rewrite of *The Sun Also Rises*, eventually finished 21 September 1925. In the novel the 'good' characters meet here:

> We [Jake Barnes, Brett Ashley, and Bill Gorton] got in the taxi. . . . 'We might as well go to the Closerie,' Brett said. . . . Sitting out on the terraces of the Lilas Brett ordered whisky and soda, and I took one, too, and Bill took another pernod. . . . Brett looked at me. 'I was a fool to go away,' she said. 'One's an ass to leave Paris.'

Hemingway and his friend John Dos Passos sat here and drank vermouth cassis and read the Old Testament together in 1924. 'The Song of Deborah and Chronicles and Kings were our favorites', claimed Dos Passos, who told Hemingway that by basing his 'wiry short sentences on cablese and the King James Bible, Hem would become the first great American stylist'. Here in the autumn of 1925, Dos Passos listened to a portion of Hemingway's *The Torrents of Spring*, written in ten days between the first and second drafts of *The Sun Also Rises*. He urged Hemingway not to publish this parody of Sherwood Anderson's *Dark Laughter*. Hemingway preferred instead to listen to the encouragement of Pauline Pfeiffer and certainly anticipated that Liveright would refuse to publish it, thus freeing him to sign with Scribner's.

It was also at this café on their second meeting (see site No. 13 for their initial meeting) that F. Scott Fitzgerald complained that his latest book *The Great Gatsby* (1925) was not selling, and he asked Hemingway to accompany him to Lyons to get a car — an unhappy but hilarious episode which is told in the longest chapter of Hemingway's memoirs.

In his semiautobiographical novel *Of Time and the River* (1935), Thomas Wolfe describes the 'priceless, rare, and uncostly pleasure and excitement of café life' that gives young Americans 'the sensation of a whole world given over without reserve or shame to pleasure'. He recreates a lengthy discussion about expatriation in the Closerie des Lilas. His alter ego Eugene Gant (who feels 'that I am a stranger here') questions Frank Starwick (who claims 'I am an American only by accident of birth, by spirit, temperament, inclination, I have always been European'):

> 'And you mean you could continue to lead this kind of life without ever growing tired of it?'
> 'What do you mean by "this kind of life"?' said Starwick.
> His friend nodded towards the crowded and noisy terrace of the café.
> 'I mean sitting around at cafés all day long, going to nightclubs — eating, drinking, sitting, — moving on from one place to another — spending your life that way.'

Starwick asserts that he finds it 'much more interesting and amusing' than a nine-to-five job 'doing useless and dreary work'. When Gant responds by asking how he can stay in a place when he does not belong and does not know the people, Starwick says,

> 'Because Paris belongs to the world — to Europe — more than it belongs to France. One does not come here because he wants to know the French: he comes because he can find here the most pleasant, graceful and civilized life on earth.'
> 'Yes, but there are other things that may be more important than leading a graceful and pleasant life.'
> 'What for instance?' said Starwick, looking at him.

'Getting your work done is one of them. For you, I should think that would be a great deal more important.'

Starwick was again silent; the old bestial grimace, image of an unutterable anguish and confusion in his soul, for a moment contorted his pleasant ruddy face, developed, passed, was gone; he said quietly and with the infinite weariness of despair that had now become the image of his life:

'Getting my work done! My God! as if it mattered.'

'There was a time when you thought it did, Frank.'

'Yes, there was a time when I did think so,' he said lifelessly.

Such scenes of struggle with expatriation and moral conflict appear in numerous fictions as well as memoirs.

William Shirer remembers that in the company of Elliot Paul and Eugene Jolas, his fellow newsmen on the *Chicago Tribune*, he sat with Pound and Hemingway at the Closerie. Pound was very talkative, arguing about the merits of the various little literary magazines in Paris. Shirer was struck by Hemingway's modesty:

Hemingway did not join in the discussion. Somewhat to my surprise, after all I had heard of him, he did not look or talk much like a writer. He was big and athletic, with a ruddy complexion and bright, lively eyes. Turning to me he began to talk of sports: the six-day bicycle races at the Velodrome d'Hiver, the fights at the Cirque de Paris and a new French middleweight boxer he thought might make it, the tennis and Suzanne Lenglen, the graceful, vivacious French champion. He was playing a lot of tennis, he said, and doing even more boxing — he was even trying to teach Ezra Pound the art. . . . I wondered how he found time to write. He said not a word about writing, which I was hoping he would, for like most of the young Americans in Paris I was already trying to write poems and short stories and finding it more difficult than I had anticipated. I had thought at first that this was a good opportunity to talk about it but, without saying so, he made it clear he did not want to touch on the subject and I was too timid to bring it up.

This old café is now mainly a restaurant. Look inside for the bar with the copper plaque with Hemingway's name on it and the picture behind the bar that will show you how the café looked in the early decades of this century. The mosaic floors, ebony wood walls, brass, little red lamps, fresh flowers, and live piano music create a warm environment. Dos Passos recalled that there was still one lilac bush in the mid 1920s. Today the only lilac is in the colour of the neon signs.

Look across the boulevard to see the Bal Bullier Brasserie on the corner. The original, Bullier Hall, was across the Avenue de l'Observatoire (now an ugly university building), as Hemingway describes it in his memoirs. This was a popular meeting place for dancing and drinking even before the 1920s. Malcolm Cowley wrote to a fellow Harvard colleague that the Bal Bullier was 'very Western Hall'. He adds that here he met Nina Hamnett, an English portrait painter, and once in the summer of 1922 got very drunk here. In the 1930s the hall became a favourite place for political meetings.

**2** **Marshal Ney statue:** corner of Boulevard du Montparnasse and Avenue de l'Observatoire 6e

In his *A Moveable Feast* Hemingway says he often sat on the Closerie des Lilas terrace 'to keep the statue company' and gaze at 'my old friend' Marshal Ney (who commanded the rear guard in Napoleon's retreat from Russia, in 1812, and was executed at this crossroads). Ford Madox Ford was fond of referring to the execution as the Sacco and Vanzetti case of its day. In 1924, Hemingway gazed at the statue, 'with his sword out and the shadows of the trees on the bronze', and thought of his friend Gertrude Stein living nearby: 'and I thought, I will do my best to serve her and see she gets justice for the good work she had done as long as I can, so help me God and Mike Ney. But the hell with her lost-generation talk and all the dirty, easy labels.'

In *The Sun Also Rises*, Jake Barnes walks from Montparnasse back to his apartment:

> I passed Ney's statue standing among the new-leaved chestnut-trees in the car-light. There was a faded purple wreath leaning against the base. I stopped and read the inscription: from the Bonapartist Groups, some date; I forget. He looked very fine, Marshal Ney in his top-boots, gesturing with his sword among the green new horse-chestnut leaves.

Statue of Marshal Ney near the Closerie des Lilas. 'My old friend', Hemingway called him.

Marshal Ney faces the Garden of Marco Polo, which is one of three gardens — the largest being the Luxembourg. Find the fountain at the entrance.

## 3  Place de l'Observatoire                                          6e

In *The Green Hills of Africa*, Hemingway describes how fine the fountains were: 'water sheen rippling on the bronze of horses' manes, bronze beasts and shoulders, green under thin-flowing water'. Today, beside an intersection of several streets loud with the noise of cars and buses, one can hear the sound of water at the entrance of the esplanade leading to the Luxembourg Gardens. This grand esplanade — from the fountain to rue Auguste-Comte — is lined on both sides with double rows of linden trees. In *A Moveable Feast* Hemingway describes the tree blossoms, the gravel walks and pigeons in this 'little Luxembourg'.

**Above** Fountain at the Place de l'Observatoire. Beyond is the Senate (Palais du Luxembourg). In *The Green Hills of Africa* Hemingway remembered the 'water seen rippling on the bronze of the horses' manes'.

**Below** Place de l'Observatoire during Hemingway's Paris days. Closerie des Lilas is off to the left; the fountain of the Marco Polo garden of the Luxembourg Gardens can be seen on the left; the Boul' Mich' is straight ahead. On the right, where now an ugly university building stands, is the Bal Bullier, one of the most famous dance halls and gardens in the nineteenth and early twentieth centuries. (Roger-*Viollet*)

Return toward the Closerie des Lilas and you will see rue Notre-Dame-des-Champs on the right. Look for the new white building on the right as you walk down the street.

**4  Hemingway's second home:** 113 rue Notre-Dame-des-Champs
6e

When Ernest and Hadley returned from Canada in 1924 with their new baby, John Hadley Nicanor (nicknamed Bumby), they found this semi-furnished (and without electricity) second-floor apartment (the present building is new) over a sawmill owned by Pierre Chautard, who rented it to them in three-month cycles. They could have afforded better, but he was tight with Hadley's money and talked often of his 'poverty', dressing the role.

In *The Green Hills of Africa*, Hemingway recalls 'the sudden whine of the saw, the smell of sawdust and the chestnut tree over the roof'. Though the whine of the saw was noisy, the Luxembourg Gardens and the Closerie des Lilas were near, Pound was up the street, Stein was four blocks away, and Beach was across the gardens. His friend Archibald MacLeish paid tribute to the Hemingway of this time and place:

> . . . the lad in the Rue de Notre Dame des Champs
> In the carpenter's loft on the left-hand side going down —
> The lad with the supple look like a sleepy panther —
> And what became of him? Fame became of him.
>
> Veteran out of the wars before he was twenty:
> Famous at twenty-five: thirty a master —
> Whittled a style for his time from a walnut stick
> In a carpenter's loft in a street of the April city.

On 10 March, after the christening of Bumby, a party was held here. Stein and Toklas, Beach and Monnier, and others enjoyed the traditional party of champagne and sugared almonds.

When Margaret Anderson and her cigar-smoking friend Jane Heap visited this apartment, Hemingway read a story of his, which they took immediately for their Exile's Number (spring 1923) of the *Little Review*. They subsequently published several more short stories and poems of his. Anderson thought that Hemingway was 'simple', instinctively generous, and 'soft-hearted'. Searching for his animal prototype, Heap observed

Ernest Hemingway in the courtyard of his second apartment, above a sawmill, in 1924, before his hair grew longer and his clothes became casual and worn. (*Princeton University Library*)

(according to Anderson), 'Hemingway is a rabbit — white and pink face, soft brown eyes that look at you without blinking. As for his love of boxing and bull-fighting — all that is thrashing up the ground with his hind feet.' Hadley, in her old clothes, they felt sorry for, as did all women visitors to this apartment.

This is the apartment that Fitzgerald tried to enter between 3 and 4 a.m. one morning in a drunken scene that ended with him urinating on the front step. He wrote Hemingway a letter of apology: 'it is only fair to say that the deplorable man who entered your apartment Saturday night was *not* me but a man named Johnston who has often been mistaken for me'.

In May, after the Hemingways moved here, William Carlos Williams, an American poet and physician (as well as a good friend of Pound and McAlmon), visited the Hemingways. Williams, as did Dos Passos, Beach, and several other friends, attended a late-afternoon bathing of Bumby. On this occasion Williams conducted a medical examination and advised that Bumby move from mother's milk to a bottle. The diagnosis must have worked for within a year Hemingway had trained Bumby to put up his fists and assume a ferocious expression.

For the first two years of their life here, the three Hemingways lived in domestic harmony. In the autumn of 1925, Hemingway bought Joan Miró's *The Farm* for Hadley's 34th birthday and hung it over their dining-room table. Later she acknowledged that the painting was 'really for himself'. During the summer of 1926, after Hadley discovered his affair with Pauline Pfeiffer, they separated and moved out of this apartment.

Nothing remains of the 'sawmill apartment' today. A new university building has replaced the flat. But at No. 110 across the street one can still find the bakery that Hemingway used to cut through — 'through the good bread smells of the ovens and the shop to the street — to the Boulevard du Montparnasse'. Take this shortcut up the stairs and through the door (closed weekends). Hadley walked through the warm bakery to practise piano in the cold basement of a music store nearby. One of their favourite local restaurants was once near the front of this bakery. (Turn left for just a few steps as you leave the bakery.)

**5  Nègre de Toulouse:** 159 Boulevard du Montparnasse          6e

Hemingway, who was acquainted with the proprietor, M. Lavigne, drank 'the good Cahors wine' here, diluting it 'about one-third with water'. It is now La Pizzeria and, naturally, does not serve the cassoulet Hemingway enjoyed. In the 1950s he remembered:

> I walked in the early dusk up the street and stopped outside the terrace of the Nègre de Toulouse restaurant where our red and white napkins were in wooden napkin rings in the napkin rack waiting for us to come to dinner. I read the menu mimeographed in purple ink and saw that the *plat du jour* was cassoulet. It made me hungry to read the name.

Harold Loeb, who admired Hemingway's 'combination of toughness and sensitivity', remembers that he, Kathleen (Kitty) Cannell, Hadley, and Ernest had a wonderful meal of lobster *a l'Américaine*, two bottles of Pouilly-Fuissé, and a brie. They talked of Ford Madox Ford. Later the Hemingways attended a farewell dinner here for Loeb and Bill Smith. Smith was Hemingway's boyhood friend from his summers in Horton Bay, Michigan. The party was given by Kitty Cannell, who thought Hemingway overacted the hairy-chested role in order to suppress his compassion and softness. She had been advising Hemingway to write longer pieces of fiction with real plots. Cannell, a friend of Loeb, worked with him on *Broom* magazine.

That night Hemingway told her he was working on 'a novel full of plot and drama'. It was *The Sun Also Rises*, using Loeb and Smith as characters. He also wrote (though did not publish) a short story about Ford Madox Ford and Stella Bowen set in the Nègre de Toulouse.

In a typical use of known experiences and place for fictional treatment, Hemingway uses this restaurant in *The Sun Also Rises*. Jack Barnes takes Georgette to 'Lavigne's restaurant'. When she sees the restaurant she dismisses it as 'no great thing of a restaurant.' Yet after dinner she concedes, 'It isn't chic, but the food is all right'.

On 24 April 1945, Hemingway wrote to his first wife, Hadley, about his 'liberation' of Paris and the Ritz. He was in his mid-40s and soon would marry his fourth wife, but this Second World War experience brought back all the memories of the places he loved in the 1920s with Hadley: 'We liberated Lipps (old man gave me a bottle of Martell) and then liberated the Negre de Toulouse'. It was, he says elsewhere in this letter, 'the wildest, most beautiful wonderful time ever ever.'

A few doors down at No. 166 lived Katherine Anne Porter, during 1932-3 after Hemingway had moved to Florida. She then moved to rue Notre-Dame-des-Champs with her husband. Her love of Paris is expressed in the words of Mary Treadwell, a character in her only novel, *Ship of Fools*, who exclaims, 'Oh God, I'm homesick. I'll never leave Paris again, I promise, if you'll let me just get there this once more. If every soul left it one day and grass grew in the pavements, it would still be Paris to me, I'd want to live there.'

In the Hôtel Vénétia (now apartments) at No. 159, briefly lived Edna St. Vincent Millay, the poet, and Harriet Monroe, editor of *Poetry*, as well as, whenever he lived in Paris, Donald Ogden Stewart — humorist and good friend of Hemingway. Hemingway stayed here 28 January to 3 February 1926, on his way from Schruns to New York City to negotiate the change of publishers he had manoeuvred.

Glance across the street to see the intersection of rue Campagne Première with the boulevard, where the original Jockey was located on the right-hand corner in a one-story building. The present Le Jockey is ahead on your walk. In an apartment at No. 137 during the 1920s lived Julian Street (*Where Paris Dines*) and Harry Leon Wilson (*Euling's Lady*). At No. 135 was the Hôtel des Etats Unis, where many foreign visitors stayed, including Sergei Eisenstein, the great Russian cinematographer in the late 1930s. Elmer Rice set his play *The Left Bank* (1931) in one of the hotels on this boulevard.

## 6 Le Jockey: 127 Boulevard du Montparnasse 6e

In 1921 the Academie du Caméléon, an art and literary cabaret, was founded on the Boulevard du Montparnasse at the east corner of rue Campagne Première in a one-storey building. In November of 1923 it was replaced by Le Jockey Club and cabaret. Early pictures show large painted figures on the outside of the building, including an Indian on an Appaloosa, and the entrance on the corner. When the Jockey moved to a one-storey building on the corner of rue de Chevreuse, it decorated the building much like the former location with large cut-out faces of people and a more static painting of an Indian on a standing horse. Apparently the club operated until the Second World War. The present café, with no trace of artistry, is named in its honour.

The original Jockey club was a popular haunt that rivalled the Dôme. Named after its founder 'Jockey' Miller, it was taken over and redecorated with cowboy scenes by Hilaire Hiler, an American painter. Hiler played the piano while Kiki (an artist's model and courtesan named Alice Prin) sang. Kiki and Man Ray, who lived just down the street, were habitués of this bar. There are many ancedotes about scenes in 'the Jockey'. Hemingway is believed to have called it the 'best' night-club 'that ever was'.

The original Jockey is synonymous with Kiki, whose suggestive songs and gestures, and whose black hose and garters against her white thighs, electrified many young visitors. One of these men, Frederick Kohner, for whom her presence in his fantasies and eventually in his bed was central to his year in Paris, called his own memoirs *Kiki of Montparnasse*. Hemingway, in his introduction to Kiki's memoirs, says of her: 'She never had a room of her own and never was a lady at any time. But for about ten years she was as close as people get nowadays to being a Queen but that, of course, is very different from being a lady.'

McAlmon tells of an incident at the original Jockey which humiliated Sinclair Lewis (*Main Street*), who earlier (1921) had been snubbed when he tried to buy drinks at the Dôme. The crowd considered him 'just a best seller' — as someone called to him across the tables. During the summer of 1923 in the Jockey, a 'tough little flapper' said 'withered carrot' within earshot of the red-headed Lewis. Flushing, the Nobel Prize winner asked, 'Do you know you are speaking to a man of international fame?' When she failed to be impressed, he left, upset. Later in an essay ('Self-Conscious America' in *The American Mercury*), Lewis got even by attacking 'the geniuses and their disciples who frequent' the cafés of Montparnasse.

Continue down Montparnasse and turn right into a narrow street beside the flower shop.

**7   George Seldes and Nathanael West:** 9 rue de la Grande Chaumière
6e

Several writers such as Nathanael West, American novelist, Samuel Beckett, Irish dramatist, and George Seldes, newspaperman, lived in the Hôtel Liberia on this street of art schools, studios, and supply shops. Note the red-brick Académie de la Grande Chaumière at No. 14 (founded in 1904) and the ateliers (studios) at Nos 10, 8, 6, and 2.

For the three months that Nathanael West was in Paris in 1926, he lived in the Hôtel Liberia. This was long before he wrote *Day of the Locust* and *Miss Lonelyhearts*. He wrote and set his first novel, *The Dream Life of Balso Snell*, in his hotel. From one of the upper windows, the pregnant Janey jumps to the street amid 'the usual crowds . . . hurrying to lunch from the Academies Colorossa and Grande Chaumière'. When her lover, Beagle, happens on the scene after the police arrive, he leaves and walks far down the Boulevard du Montparnasse to drink in a café in Avenue du Maine. This brief, surrealist novel satirizing a phoney bohemian life was the last book published by McAlmon's Contact Publishing firm.

If West did not encounter Hemingway, George Seldes certainly did. They both were reporting the Genoa Conference in 1919 and, with Lincoln Steffens, met every night in a bar or trattoria. Seldes claims it was during this trip that Hemingway learned cablese and pronounced it a 'new language'. Later they were both in Madrid covering the war, Seldes for the *Chicago Tribune*. During a period of his 14 years living in and visiting Paris, Seldes lived at the Liberia. He describes the hotel as cheap then, with bathrooms at the end of the corridors and no telephone (the concierge yelled up the stairs if a visitor came). The Sélect was his regular café.

**8   Saint Luke's Episcopal Church:** 5 rue de la Grande-Chaumière
6e

On 16 March 1924 John 'Bumby' Hemingway was christened at the American Chapel of Saint Luke with Gertrude Stein and Eric Edward 'Chink' Dorman-Smith as godparents. Dorman-Smith, Hemingway's war buddy, made the arrangements with the minister. Bumby was dressed in a lace-trimmed robe that had been worn by his father almost 25 years before. The church, now gone, was just around the corner from the Pound apartment in rue Notre-Dame-des-Champs.

Before you turn left at Notre-Dame-des-Champs, look to the right, where Ford Madox Ford lived at No. 84, straight ahead, in the tan building with curved supports beneath the windows. In his memoirs, Hemingway describes an unpleasant encounter with Ford ('the heavy, wheezing ignoble presence of Ford') at the Closerie des Lilas. McAlmon thought Ford could 'double for Lord Plushbottom'.

**9  Ezra Pound:** 70 bis Notre-Dame-des-Champs          6e

The rear garden or *pavillon* apartment where Pound lived with his wife Dorothy was, as Hemingway described it, 'as poor as Gertrude Stein's studio was rich. It had good light and was heated by a stove and it had paintings by Japanese artists that Ezra knew.' The apartment looked like an art gallery and held furniture made by Pound.

Initially, Hemingway distrusted Pound because of his bohemian dress, but soon he was calling Pound 'generous and really noble'. The Hemingways had tea with the Pounds during their early months in Paris in 1922. The younger writer (23), thought the older man (37) was 'a sort of saint' who was 'kinder and more christian about people than I was'. Hadley claimed that Ernest 'listened at Pound's feet as to an oracle' — the oracle drank 17 cups of tea that visit. Pound delivered his monologue with his unclipped goatee jutting out in front of him.

Pound learned to box with Hemingway, talked to him about clarity of style and freedom from 'emotional slither', and introduced him to many writers. Hemingway met Wyndham Lewis, Ernest Walsh, and Malcolm Cowley in this apartment. Pound, who had been a leader in literary circles in London, continued to encourage young writers in Paris. His friendship with Hemingway is evident in the following extract from a letter (9 March 1922) that Hemingway wrote (with boxing slang) to Sherwood Anderson, less than three months after he and Hadley had arrived in Paris:

> Pound took six of my poems and sent them wit a letter to Thayer, Scofield [*Dial*], that is, you've heard of him maybe. Pound thinks I'm a swell poet. He also took a story for the Little Review. I've been teaching Pound to box wit little success. He habitually leads wit his chin and has the general grace of the crayfish or crawfish. He's willing but short winded. Going over there this afternoon for another session

but there aint much job in it as I have to shadow box between rounds to get up a sweat. Pound sweats well, though, I'll say that for him. Besides it's pretty sporting of him to risk his dignity and his critical reputation at something that he don't know nothing about. He's really a good guy, Pound, wit a fine bitter tongue onto him. He's written a good review of Ulysses for April Dial.

They were a better match at tennis, which they played regularly in 1923.

Pound was unsuccessful with Hemingway's poems at *The Dial*, but he urged Ford Madox Ford to use the young Hemingway as his assistant editor for the *Transatlantic Review*: 'he writes very good verse and he's the finest prose stylist in the world . . . He's disciplined, too.'

The poet Ralph Cheever Dunning lived in this building and was nurtured by Pound. Hemingway paints a picture of the opium-smoking Dunning — 'an agent of evil' — in *A Moveable Feast*. The Hemingways were going to stay in Pound's apartment (Pound was in Rapallo, Italy) and keep an eye on Dunning when they first returned from Toronto, but the concierge would not let them in. Soon they found an apartment just down the street over a sawmill.

In *A Moveable Feast* Hemingway describes leaving the Pound apartment and walking toward his sawmill apartment, 'looking down the high-sided street to the opening at the end where the bare trees showed'.

Hemingway met Henry 'Mike' Strater here. While they were sipping whiskey out of teacups, they discovered that they both loved to box and were soon meeting regularly to spar. Strater, a painter and a graduate of Princeton, was six feet and 14 stone. He painted the first portrait of Hemingway. When Strater, a long-time friend, was later asked if Hemingway were shy, he responded, 'shy like one of those police dogs.'

Margaret Anderson and Jane Heap, just over from New York, went first to visit Ezra Pound, who had become the European editor of their *Little Review* in 1917. Anderson discovered that, in person, Pound was nervous, self-conscious, and agitated, reminding her of a 'large baby performing its repertoire of physical antics'. After an hour in his studio, she felt that she 'had been sitting through a human experiment in a behaviorist laboratory'. Though she liked him, she found him sexist ('the tendency to orientalize one's attitude toward women'), a fault she thought was intensified in American men by expatriation.

Pound left Paris in 1924 to break new ground in Italy. Paris was too crowded by then, he claimed. According to Pound,

The new lot of American *émigrés* were anything but the Passionate Pilgrims of James' day or the enquirers of my own. We came to find something, to learn, possibly to conserve, but this lot came in disgust.

Later, Katherine Anne Porter moved to No. 70 bis in 1934. She describes her apartment as having 'six rooms on three floors, two baths, and central heating [and] a little closed garden full of shrubs and ivy-covered walls'. While here Porter continued to write fiction and to translate a French book into English.

Wind down the Notre-Dame-des-Champs (away from Hemingway's sawmill home). Unfortunately, many of the old studios have been replaced by ugly buildings. For Pound and other Americans, this street was made famous by James MacNeill Whistler, whose Académie Whistler was at No. 60 on the left (and his studio at No. 86). Pound once called Whistler 'our only artist'. At No. 59 on the right (now a new building) was Hôtel Printania, where McAlmon stayed briefly in the mid-1920s. Turn left into rue Vavin and walk past the little park and corner studios. Do not miss a full view of the tiled building at No. 26 on the right. Rue Vavin crosses Boulevard Raspail. You will pass No. 50 rue Vavin, where Harold Stearns lived. Louise Bryant (widowed by John Reed, divorced by William Bullitt) was living in his hotel when she died.

When you reach the Boulevard Montparnasse and see the four famous cafés facing each other, you are looking at the centre of small-town life in the 1920s. If you can imagine most of the cars gone, you will see how easy it was for the artists to move from one place to the other each night. The Rotonde is on your left, opposite the Dôme; the Sélect is on your right, opposite the Coupole. Turn left to visit the Rotonde. At this intersection (Place Vavin) was the original summit of the Parnassus 'mound'.

## 10  La Rotonde: 103 Boulevard du Montparnasse                6e

'It may be said that from 1910 to 1920, the Rotonde was one of the best known places on earth', wrote Léon-Paul Fargue, a French poet and member of Odéonia. Opened in 1911 at No. 105, Café de la Rotonde took over the Café du Parnasse (next-door) in 1924. 'No matter what café in Montparnasse you ask a taxi driver to bring you to from the right bank of the river, they always take you to the Rotonde', says Hemingway's Jake Barnes.

La Rotonde is conveniently located by métro Vavin at the intersection of Boulevards Raspail and Montparnasse, which is why Jake, in *The Sun Also Rises*, says that no matter what café you ask a taxi-driver to bring you to, 'they always take you to the Rotonde'. The original La Coupole is across the street (under the métro sign).

When he first came to Paris, in a by-line for the *Toronto Star Weekly* ('American Bohemia in Paris'), Hemingway was critical of the Rotonde of the 1920s where the 'scum of Greenwich Village' congregate:

> It is a strange-acting and strange-looking breed that crowd the tables of the Café Rotonde. They have all striven so hard for a careless individuality of clothing that they have achieved a sort of uniformity of eccentricity. A first look into the smoky, high-ceilinged, table-crammed interior of the Rotonde gives the same feeling that hits you as you step into a bird house at the zoo.

Before long, he too was wearing his hair long and sitting in cafés. According to Michael Reynolds, 'He became what, at first, he most despised'. Perhaps Robert McAlmon had Hemingway's early sarcasm in mind when he commented on the critics of the Rotonde:

> As summer came, crossing and recrossing between the Dôme and the Rotonde on an evening . . . anybody from the writing or art world of any country was apt to appear and quite as apt to be dead drunk or mildly intoxicated: I know that many of them betray their own strong or weak moments, as you wish to call them. They went back to their own countries — the Americans were the worst — and wrote righteous and moralizing articles and editorials on expatriate life on the continent. Such articles always disgust me, because

knowing London and her pubs, New York and her speak-easies, as well as Paris, I see no use in the lousy pretence that people who drink don't drink elsewhere than in Paris.

Among the very few patrons of the Rotonde who mention the food is Edna St. Vincent Millay who in 1922 ate a daily lunch of *choucroute garnie*, which she described as 'fried sauerkraut trimmed with boiled potatoes, a large slice of ham and a fat hot dog, — yum, yum, werry excillient'.

Before turning to the Sélect, note the statue of Balzac by Rodin in the middle of Boulevard Raspail next to the Rotonde.

## 11  Le Sélect: 99 Boulevard du Montparnasse                    6e

'Cafe Select,' [Jake Barnes] told the driver. 'Boulevard Montparnasse.' We drive straight down, turning around the Lion de Belfort [Place Denfert-Rochereau] that guards the passing Montrouge trams. Brett looked straight ahead. On the Boulevard Raspail, with the lights of Montparnasse in sight, Brett said: 'Would you mind very much if I asked you to do something?'
'Don't be silly.'
'Kiss me just once more before we get there.'

The Sélect, at the corner of rue Vavin, was perhaps the most popular café in the 1920s. Here was where Hart Crane picked a fight with a waiter and landed in jail, where he was to languish for a full week. Today the Sélect is still filled with expatriates, lovers and tourists. Coffee on the terrace now costs 9 francs.

Margaret Anderson remembers Hemingway showing up at the Sélect every morning, pushing through the terrace chairs 'like a prowling animal' looking for a particular friend. Morley Callaghan also remembers being at the Sélect with Hemingway, when the latter introduced him to Joan Miró. However, in *A Moveable Feast*, Hemingway claims he shuns the 'vice and the collective instinct' of the 'collection of inmates' at the Sélect and crosses the boulevard to the Dôme, where 'there were people . . . who worked'. These words do not describe the present customers, but his remark reveals the strong preferences that individuals had for particular cafés.

Harold Stearns, who appears as the inebriated Harvey Stone in Hemingway's *The Sun Also Rises* and as the investigator Wiltshire Tobin

Writing on the terrace of the Sélect or playing chess in the back are honoured traditions. Unfortunately for him, Hart Crane was doing neither when he punched the director of the Sélect and was arrested, beaten, and imprisoned for a week before Harry Crosby bailed him out.

in Kay Boyle's *Monday Night*, was a regular at the Sélect. Kay Boyle, a fiction writer from Minnesota who lived abroad for 18 years, describes meeting him with Robert McAlmon:

> There at the Sélect that night was Harold Stearns, the Peter Pickem of the Paris edition of the Chicago *Tribune*, Bob told me, who picked the winners at the race course at Maisons Lafitte (or else failed to pick them). He was standing drinking at the bar, with a brown felt hat set, in a shabby parody of respectability, quite high on his head.

She noted his frayed collar, dirty ears, unshaved face, and black finger-nails; yet after he began to speak, she adds, 'I never questioned the truth of every word he said'. This tribute is recorded in one of her alternative chapters to McAlmon's reprinted *Being Geniuses Together.*

> [Jake Barnes] walked past the sad tables of the Rotonde to the Select. There were a few people inside at the bar, and outside, alone, sat Harvey Stone. He had a pile of saucers in front of him, and he needed a shave.
> 'Sit down,' said Harvey, 'I've been looking for you.'
> 'What's the matter?'
> 'Nothing? Just looking for you.'
> 'Been out to the races?'
> 'No. Not since Sunday.'
> 'What do you hear from the States?'

'Nothing. Absolutely nothing.'
'What's the matter?'
'I don't know. I'm through with them. I'm absolutely through with them.'
He leaned forward and looked me in the eye.
'Do you want to know something, Jake?'
'Yes.'
'I haven't had anything to eat for five days.'

Jake lends Stone 100 francs. The real-life Stearns and the fictional 'expatriates' of Hemingway's novel did much to create the mythology of the intoxicated artist of Montparnasse.

Hemingway was generous in his loans to Stearns. An astute observer of history and civilization, but a man who almost went to pieces in Paris, Stearns was a central figure here during the time when, as he describes it, the Dôme was 'just an old-fashioned corner bistro', La Coupole 'an old coal-and-wood yard', the Rotonde a 'small and dirty and historical' café, and the Dingo a 'tiny workmen's cafe'.

On 29 August 1926 in the *Paris Tribune*, Elliot Paul — newspaperman, writer, and café-goer — declared:

> The Montparnassians sleep in the morning and in the afternoon and spend the evening and the neo-evening, up to the rising hour for ashmen and concierges, upon the terraces of the Dôme, the Rotonde, the Select, and other neighboring cafés. They have dark circles under their eyes, have read parts of *Ulysses*, and are likely to be self-made Freudians.

According to William Shirer, a *Tribune* newsman, the Sélect was where Isadora Duncan's demonstration in support of Sacco and Vanzetti began. Duncan got into a 'violent discussion' with Floyd Gibbons, a legendary war correspondent of the *Chicago Tribune* who had lost an eye at Château-Thierry and wore a black patch. When Gibbons claimed that the two Italian anarchists were given a 'fair trial', Isadora became furious and gave Gibbons a 'tongue-lashing'. Soon 'sympathizers on both sides joined in and there was a fray with glasses and saucers hurled about until the police intervened to break it up'. Because Sacco and Vanzetti were scheduled to be executed in Boston that very evening, Isadora could not calm down.

It was begining to rain, says Shirer, but undaunted she set off down the Boulevard Raspail, followed by a small crowd, and marched on for two miles to the American Embassy, on the other side of the Seine. There before the locked gates of the Embassy, guarded by a platoon of steel-helmeted gendarmes, she held high a burning taper and kept a silent vigil in the chilling drizzle for the rest of the night. At dawn an American reporter arrived and informed her that the executions had again been put off. 'Thank God!' Isadora sighed and quietly left. Later, when Sacco and Vanzetti were indeed put to death, rioting broke out around Paris and crowds stormed the American Embassy.

A third newspaperman, George Seldes, recalls talking here in the 1930s about Spain with Hemingway and Robert Desnos, a French Surrealist poet who would later die in a concentration camp. They adjourned to Desnos's apartment in the rue de Seine, where they were joined by several other newsmen and talked until dawn about the threat to Spain and Europe from Fascism and the distortions of the press.

> As we stumbled (more from lack of sleep than alcohol) down the staircase from the Desnos apartment to the street, Hemingway turned to us and said: 'And I had to go to Spain before you liberal bastards would believe that I was on your side'.

When you cross the street to the Coupole, you move from the 6th to the 14th arrondissement. The cobblestone street was tarred in 1987.

## 12  La Coupole: 102–4 Boulevard du Montparnasse               14e

Opened December 1927, this brasserie was a favourite night-spot and dance hall in a two-storey building. It became the hang-out of Kiki, the famous model–mistress. Until 14 April 1988 it was probably the most interesting of the Montparnasse cafés because it had not been remodelled. However, it was razed by a new owner, who reportedly stored all paintings, columns, and traditional furnishings with promises to 'restore' the historic brasserie.

Léon-Paul Fargue said that La Coupole was a 'sidewalk academy' where poets and painters learned 'Bohemian life, scorn for the middle classes, humor and how to hold a glass'.

**Above** Magic lights of La Coupole on a wet night. The favourite brasserie of Montparnasse since 1928. The building was destroyed in 1988. (*Roger-Viollet*)

**Right** Inside La Coupole in about 1930. 'The tables are full — they are always full — someone is moved down and crowded together, something is knocked over, more people come in at the swinging door', writes Hemingway of café life. (*Roger-Viollet*)

One young man from Montreal who learned his academy lessons in 1928 was John Glassco (*Memoirs of Montparnasse*), who met Hemingway here. Glassco was drinking with McAlmon, whose 'capacity for alcohol was astounding: within the next half-hour he drank half a dozen whiskies with no apparent effect'. When Hemingway approached the table the two Americans exchanged insults:

'If it isn't Ernest, the fabulous phony! How are the bulls?'
'And how is North American McAlmon, the unfinished poem?'
He leaned over and pummelled McAlmon in the ribs, grinning and blowing beery breath over the table.

Walk up Boulevard du Montparnasse in the direction of the Rotonde and the Dôme.

**13  Café du Dôme:** 108 Boulevard du Montparnasse                    14e

Malcolm Cowley called the Dôme, Sélect, and Rotonde the 'heart and nervous system of the . . . literary colony'. Truly this was the busiest social intersection. Such places, wrote Hemingway, 'anticipated the columnists as the daily substitutes for immortality'. He remembers that the drinks were cheap and prices 'were clearly marked on the saucers'. William Carlos Williams, in his semiautobiographical novel, *A Voyage to Pagany* (1928), describes the 'certain type of international Dôme face . . . a sort of wry face, a little on parade. There was little vivacity apparent in anyone.' Yet in his *Autobiography*, Williams mentions stopping into this café often. In the street in front he met Hemingway, 'a young man with a boil on his seat, just back from a bicycle ride in Spain'. Williams, who took only two trips to Paris during the 1920s because he was suspicious of expatriation for an artist, met several times with the Hemingways. They played tennis together and attended the prize fights. When one of the boxers got bloody, Mrs Williams pounded on the back of Ogden Nash, who was sitting in front of them, and screamed, 'Kill him! Kill him!' Williams was horrified and astonished, though she was probably aping Hemingway.

The Dôme, now a rather up-market fish restaurant as well as an enclosed *café-terrasse*, presides over the busy Place Vavin. During their first afternoons in Paris in December 1921, Ernest and Hadley warmed themselves by the charcoal braziers on the terrace of the Dôme. Here Hemingway wrote to Anderson:

> Well here we are. And we sit outside the Dome Cafe, opposite the Rotunde that's being redecorated, warmed up against one of those charcoal brazziers and it's so damned cold outside and the brazier makes it so warm and we drink rum punch, hot, and the rhum enters into us like the Holy Spirit.

Within a few years this cold, unknown newspaperman had friends and a growing reputation. Nathan Asch, according to Malcolm Cowley, describes the early recognition of Hemingway:

> I heard there [Dôme] in the early spring of 1923 that a young man

Café du Dôme during Hemingway's days in Paris. Malcolm Cowley called this intersection 'the heart and nervous system of the American Literary Colony'. (*Roger-Viollet*)

named Hemingway, who sometimes came to the Dôme for his morning coffee, was writing a new kind of very short stories and showed them to people in manuscript, or sometimes read them aloud. Some thought they were marvelous, some held their noses.

Before long the Hemingway reputation was established, according to Cowley:

> It was an event of the evening if he passed the Dôme tall, broad, and handsome, usually wearing a patched jacket and sneakers and often walking on the balls of his feet like a boxer. Arms waved in greeting from the sidewalk tables and friends ran out to urge him to sit with them.

Pound had introduced Hemingway to Cowley in the summer of 1923. More than a decade afterwards Cowley wrote his poem 'Hunter', later called 'Ernest' and collected in *Blue Juniata* (1968). Cowley would also edit *The Portable Hemingway* in 1944.

In addition to meeting Hemingway at the Dôme, Cowley claims he also met Sinclair Lewis and Ford Madox Ford there. He met Lewis in the summer of 1921, when Cowley had arrived on an American Field Service Fellowship to study French. In the winter of 1922 Cowley met Ford, whom he thought 'pathetic and sympathetic' as well as 'charming'. Ford 'adores Ezra Pound and believes that everything living in English literature comes, like Pound, from America'.

Among the fictional references to the Dôme in Hemingway's works is the following from 'Mr and Mrs Elliot':

> So they all sat around the Café du Dôme, avoiding the Rotonde across the street because it is always so full of foreigners, for a few days and then the Elliots rented a chateau in Touraine through an advertisement in the *New York Herald*.

The terrace and interior of the Dôme were remodelled again in 1986. Numerous pictures of its famous French patrons of the past can be seen inside. Walk around the corner of the Dôme into rue Delambre, passing the fresh fish stand (one of the best in Paris) and the stained-glass windows of the bar of the Dôme.

**14 Edward Titus and Samuel Putnam:** 4 and 8 rue Delambre
14e

Rue Delambre is a street crowded with former addresses of painters, sculptors, and writers. Very near the Dôme are two such addresses. In 1924, Edward Titus, a Polish-born American from New Orleans, opened a rare book room and gallery here (he had lived upstairs since 1918) called At the Sign of the Black Manikin. Two years later, under this same name, he began publishing books (Crete printer was conveniently located at No. 24 up the street). Among the 25 books he published until 1932 was the expanded English version of *Kiki's Memoirs*, translation by Samuel Putnam and foreword by Hemingway, who called it untranslatable. In 1929 he took over the defunct *This Quarter* magazine, which had published Hemingway's 'The Undefeated'. All this literary activity was financed by his wife, Helena Rubinstein, who lived elsewhere. In her opinion his literary friends were 'wasters', 'meshugga', including Hemingway, who was 'a loud-mouth and a show-off'.

Titus was assisted in the editing of *This Quarter* in 1930 by Samuel Putnam, who lived for that season at No. 8 with his wife and baby. Putnam was from Chicago and supported his life in the inexpensive suburbs of Paris from 1927 to 1933 by translating works by French and Italian writers. They left this tiny apartment behind the Coupole, whose kitchen provided them 'with an orchestral accompaniment', when Titus refused to support Putnam's enthusiasm for fellow-Chicagoan James Farrell. In *Paris Was*

*Our Mistress*, an intelligent and perceptive memoir, Putnam claims that Hemingway's *The Sun Also Rises* marked the cleavage between the earlier 'exiles' and the 'younger, unscarred generation', chronicled by Henry Miller's *Tropic of Cancer.*

**15  Le Dingo** (now L'Auberge du Centre): 10 rue Delambre    14e

Hemingway, 25 years old and not yet a published novelist, met Fitzgerald, 29 years old and at the peak of his career, at the Dingo bar and restaurant. It was late in April of 1925. Fitzgerald had earlier recommended Hemingway to Max Perkins, his editor at Scribner's, after reading the Hemingway stories published by McAlmon. Fitzgerald approached Hemingway to meet him, where the latter was drinking with two Montparnasse regulars named Duff Twysden and Pat Guthrie, who would be portrayed as Brett Ashley and Mike Campbell in *The Sun Also Rises.* Twysden was tall and thin with very short blond hair; Guthrie had the face of a heavy drinker. They were both cousins and lovers. Hemingway was attracted to Twysden, who could drink and swear with the best of them.

Fitzgerald, already tight according to Hemingway's account, ordered champagne. To Hemingway's embarrassment, the Minnesota writer highly praised his Nick Adams stories. It was a case of hero worship, and Hemingway immediately assumed the superior role. Hemingway was a husky and casually dressed man who talked little about his own writing. He thought that Fitzgerald had a 'delicate' Irish mouth and a face 'between

The Dingo Bar is now called L'Auberge du Centre, but the bar at which Fitzgerald met Hemingway late in April 1925 remains.

handsome and pretty'. The frail and elegantly dressed Fitzgerald soon turned white and nearly passed out from the champagne. He had to be taken home in a taxi.

Hemingway used the Dingo in his setting for 'A Sea Change'. In *The Sun Also Rises*, Brett and Mike, who are staying in a hotel on this street, meet Jake at the Dingo before going to Spain:

> 'I say,' said Mike, 'I'm going to the barber's.'
> 'I must bathe,' said Brett. 'Walk up to the hotel with me, Jake. Be a good chap.'
> 'We have got the loveliest hotel,' Mike said, 'I think it's a brothel!'
> 'We left our bags here at the Dingo when we got in, and they asked us at this hotel if we wanted a room for the afternoon only. Seemed frighfully pleased we were going to stay all night.'
> 'I believe it's a brothel,' Mike said. 'And I should know.'
> 'Oh, shut it and go and get your hair cut.'
> Mike went out. Brett and I sat on at the bar.
> 'Have another?'
> 'Might.'
> 'I needed that,' Brett said.
> We walked up the Rue Delambre.

The Dingo (the Crazy Man) was famous for its barman, Jimmy, from Liverpool, who served corn-beef and cabbage, real American soup, and thick beefsteaks. One can still drink *fine à l'eau* at the original bar. (Jimmy later moved to the Falstaff.)

According to Robert McAlmon, Flossie Martin and Nina Hamnett were the 'stage directors' of the Dingo and the Dôme. Hemingway called Martin, a red-head who weighed close to 14 stone, 'the girl who can always be depended on to shout obscenities'.

Halsey and Mercado, the two American university professors in Harold Loeb's second novel, *The Professors Like Vodka*, visit the Dingo for drinks. Halsey is based on Loeb's friend Bill Smith, in part the prototype for Bill Gorton in *The Sun Also Rises*; Mercado is based on Loeb himself after the legendary 1925 Pamplona Fiesta. One day Halsey meets 'Harold Stearns and discusses the effects of prohibition on the younger intellectuals'. Soon they are joined by others, and someone begins 'pounding out a popular tune on the piano'. Loeb recreates the café life rather well.

On this street in various hotels at various times in the 1920s lived Isadora

Duncan, Jo Davidson, Tristan Tzara, Harold Stearns, Man Ray, Jane Heap, John Glassco, Robert McAlmon, and Mina Loy.

Continue up rue Delambre to the Boulevard Edgar-Quinet intersection and take the first right into rue du Montparnasse. The Falstaff is down the street on your left.

## 16  Le Falstaff: 42 rue du Montparnasse                    14e

In the late 1920s, Jimmy the Barman of the Dingo moved here to the Falstaff with his famous customers. His memoirs, *This Must Be The Place* (1934), were introduced by Hemingway and 'edited' (written) by Morrill Cody, an American journalist. It was quieter than the Dingo, claims John Glassco, who describes the 'contrast between its rather stuffy oak panelling and padded seats and the haphazard way it was run by the bartender Jimmy Charters'. Note the dark wood interior and the huge copper draught beer machine. This bar and restaurant is still smaller and cosier than the crowded pavement terraces around the corner in Montparnasse.

Morley Callaghan (*That Summer in Paris*) came here in 1929 with Hemingway and Fitzgerald. One night the three men drank here with

The Falstaff, on rue du Montparnasse, remains an English oak-panelled bar and restaurant. Hemingway often dropped in to meet his friend Jimmy Charters, former light-weight fighter then bartender.

strained joviality following a boxing match between Hemingway and Callaghan in which Fitzgerald forgot to call time out until Hemingway hit the mat.

Callaghan, who would become one of Canada's best short-story writers, also tells a story of McAlmon urging him to go to the Falstaff late one evening. Callaghan soon learned he was to play bodyguard for McAlmon when a six-foot Swede named Jorgenson appeared: 'There he is,' McAlmon whispered . . . 'I had trouble with him last night in the Dingo. He said he'd be in here at ten tonight to beat me up — if I came.' After a talk with Jimmy and a few derisive grins in their direction, Jorgenson left the bar, much to the relief of McAlmon. 'Around the Quarter,' adds Callaghan, 'indignities, bitter or comical, were shared so frequently they became little more than part of the daily gossip.'

Late in the summer of 1929, Loretto and Morley Callaghan were sitting on the terrace of the Sélect before leaving Paris:

> Loretto said idly, 'Paris is lovely. We've been so happy here. But doesn't it strike you that this neighbourhood is now like a small town for us?'
>
> 'Yes, the same faces always in the same places. And all the gossip. What do you say if we go to London?'

End your walk here, for the Sphinx brothel and the Murphy studio are gone, but they are worth mentioning because they complete the picture of the social scene of the 1920s and Hemingway's activities in this quarter. However, if you wish to visit their sites, return to Boulevard Edgar-Quinet and turn right for the brothel, or left for the Murphy studio, down the west side of the cemetery.

## 17  Le Sphinx: 31 Boulevard Edgar-Quinet                                14e

Though now gone, the Sphinx was the most famous brothel of the Montparnasse area. In his *Paris Was Our Mistress*, Samuel Putnam describes the grand opening of the chromium-plated brothel, to which all the 6th arrondissement seemed to be invited ('and we were supposed to bring our wives!'). After the free champagne, Madame gave a tour of the *bar américain* and the rooms with bidets, and introduced her young girls who would entertain 'les artistes'. The few visiting married couples who attended found the event 'charmingly risqué', according to Putnam.

In 1930, Henry Miller lived conveniently nearby (around the corner toward the cemetery), in an apartment overlooking the square at No. 1 bis rue du Maine. 'I got a little rake-off, for writing the pamphlets', he says in *Tropic of Cancer*. 'That is to say, a bottle of champagne and a free fuck in one of the Egyptian rooms.' He also got a commission for bringing in clients.

The Sphinx, located on this street named after a nineteenth-century historian, was decorated inside and out with huge Egyptian figures. It has been replaced by a new building housing, among others, a medical doctor and an acupuncturist, who now offer another kind of relief to artists and weary travellers.

Next-door to the Sphinx was the major Paris setting for Thomas Wolfe's *Of Time and the River* — a studio in which lived three friends (Frank, Ann, and Elinor) of Eugene Gant. Also on this street (at the other end) was the Gipsy Bar, which John Glassco describes as 'full of hardfaced young lesbians and desperate looking old women whose spotted, sinewy arms rattled with jewelled bracelets'.

**18 Gerald Murphy studio:** 69 rue Froidevaux                    14e

Gerald Murphy lent Hemingway his fifth-floor studio opposite the Montparnasse cemetery and deposited $400 into his account to help him over a difficult time. This was August of 1926 when he and Hadley were setting up separate apartments. Jed Kiley and John Peale Bishop visited him here. Hemingway actually worked here and at the Closerie des Lilas, correcting proofs of *The Sun Also Rises*, but spent most of his time in Pauline's apartment on the Right Bank. He also hung around Archibald MacLeish's apartment in rue du Bac. While he was living here he wrote 'A Canary for One'.

If you wish to visit the Montparnasse cemetery ask at the office (Edgar-Quinet entrance) for 'Index Sommaire des Célébrités'. There is among all the better-known grave sites (Tristan Tzara, Charles Baudelaire, Alfred Dreyfus, Constantin Brancusi, Jean-Paul Sartre, Simone de Beauvoir, Guy de Maupassant, and the America film actress Jean Seberg), the grave of Frederic Auguste Bartholdi (1834–1904), who designed the Statue of Liberty. This French-made statue, which stands in the New York harbour, welcomes immigrants to America — as Montparnasse and its bright cafés beckoned the Americans in the 1920s.

# 7

# HEMINGWAY'S RIGHT BANK FROM THE OPÉRA TO THE TUILERIES

Charlie directed his taxi to the Avenue de l'Opéra, which was out of his way. But he wanted to see the blue hour spread over the magnificent facade, and imagine that the cab horns, playing endlessly the first few bars of *Le Plus que Lent*, were the trumpets of the Second Empire.

Fitzgerald's 'Babylon Revisited'

The Right Bank represented the flush times for Ernest Hemingway — from the first Christmas dinner at the Café de la Paix (when he did not have enough money to pay the bill) to the last decades of his life, when success and fame bought him meals in the finest restaurants and rooms at the Ritz.

The Right Bank also held, as it still does, those institutions that tie the foreigner to his material needs. For Hemingway and other Americans, these institutions were the American Express, the American Hospital, the American Embassy, the banks, Brentanos, and that umbilical cord to home — the newspapers. Chief among the **American newspapers**, whose locations are given on **maps F and G**, were:

1    *Paris Herald* (European Edition of the *New York Herald Tribune*) 1887-1940
2    *Paris Tribune* (*Chicago Tribune*, European Edition) 1917-1934
3    *Paris Times*, 1924-1929 (no connection to the *New York Times*)

Hemingway, who wrote for the *Toronto Star* until 1923, had many friends among the American newspapermen who worked on the Right Bank and lived on the Left Bank. Like Hemingway, Henry James for a while (1875-6) earned his living in journalism, contributing a monthly Paris letter to the

*New York Tribune.* Jake Barnes, the protagonist in *The Sun Also Rises*, is a newspaperman who works here on the Right Bank and lives on the Boulevard Saint-Michel on the Left Bank.

Although the former newspaper locations are no longer worth a visit, there are a number of other locations that continue to bustle with noisy activity or mirror quiet elegance. Harry's New York Bar and the bar at the Ritz are still open. Americans still crowd Brentanos and American Express. In the shop windows or the lobby of the Ritz, you can recapture the world of Fitzgerald, whom Malcolm Cowley called the 'ambassador of literature to that Paris of the rich'.

Begin this walk with a drink on the terrace of the Café de la Paix. Coffee at 14 francs will rent a seat for several hours. If you choose not to stop at the café and have emerged from the métro stop, remain on one of the islands in the middle of the street for a broad perspective. Facing the Opéra, the National Musical Academy, you will have the Café de la Paix on your left; behind you the avenue runs down to the Comédie-Française and the Louvre.

## 1  Café de la Paix: 5 Place de l'Opéra 9e

Ernest and Hadley Hemingway spent the Christmas of 1921 walking the streets of Paris, including the length of the Avenue de l'Opéra. It was their first month in Paris and they wanted to celebrate the holiday and their good fortune to be in Paris by eating an elegant meal in the Café de la Paix, at the corner of Boulevard des Capucines and Avenue de l'Opéra. The bill that covered their fine meal exceeded their cash supply and Ernest had to run all the way back across the river to the Hôtel Jacob to get extra money. Hadley nervously waited at their table until he returned.

Café de la Paix is an important setting in Hemingway's 'My Old Man', a short story told by the son of a jockey. The boy and his father often sit out in front of the café and watch the 'streams of people going by and all sorts of guys come up and want to sell you things, and I loved to sit there with my old man'. His old man drinks a lot, and whiskey 'cost five francs, and that meant a good tip when the saucers were counted up'.

A recent echo of this short story appears in Jack 'Bumby' Hemingway's memoir of life 'with and without Papa': 'I especially liked going to the Right Bank when Papa or mother would have to go to the Guaranty Trust Company to cash a check, since we would inevitably stop for a treat at the Café de la Paix near the Opéra'.

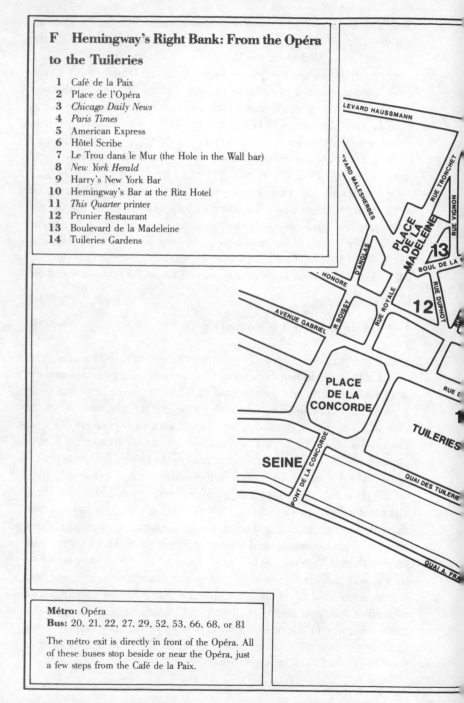

### F Hemingway's Right Bank: From the Opéra to the Tuileries

1 Café de la Paix
2 Place de l'Opéra
3 *Chicago Daily News*
4 *Paris Times*
5 American Express
6 Hôtel Scribe
7 Le Trou dans le Mur (the Hole in the Wall bar)
8 *New York Herald*
9 Harry's New York Bar
10 Hemingway's Bar at the Ritz Hotel
11 *This Quarter* printer
12 Prunier Restaurant
13 Boulevard de la Madeleine
14 Tuileries Gardens

**Métro:** Opéra
**Bus:** 20, 21, 22, 27, 29, 52, 53, 66, 68, or 81

The métro exit is directly in front of the Opéra. All of these buses stop beside or near the Opéra, just a few steps from the Café de la Paix.

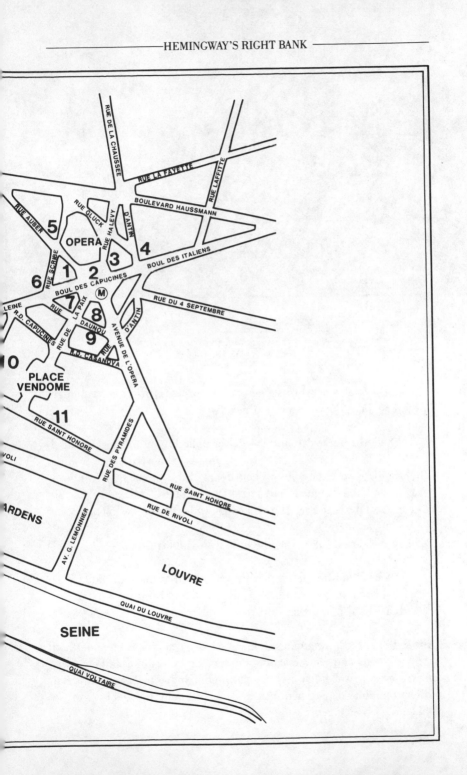

Grand Hôtel and Café de la Paix as they looked 17 years before
Ernest and Hadley Hemingway had Christmas dinner here in 1921. 'I
loved to sit there with my old man', says the young narrator of
Hemingway's 'My Old Man'.

Hemingway also sets two scenes of *The Sun Also Rises* here, though
in the first Jake Barnes merely drives by:

> I hailed a horse-cab and the driver pulled up at the curb. Settled
> back in the slow, smoothly rolling *fiacre* we moved up the Avenue
> de l'Opéra, passed the locked doors of the shops, their windows
> lighted, the Avenue broad and shiny and almost deserted. The cab
> passed the New York Herald bureau with the window full of clocks.

Later in the novel, Jake visits the café with Robert Cohn:

> After we finished the lunch we walked up to the Café de la Paix
> and had coffee. I could feel Cohn wanted to bring up Brett again,
> but I held him off it.

About 1923, E. E. Cummings, John Dos Passos, and Gilbert Seldes had
'long bibulous and conversational dinners' at the Café de la Paix. One
night they were walking from here after midnight toward a Left Bank bar
when Cummings paused to urinate and was promptly arrested by 'a whole
phalanx' of policemen.

Through the café and hotel above it seem awash only in tourists, they have a rich history. Among those attending the soirée that inaugurated the Grand Hôtel on 5 May 1862, were many famous artists, from Zola to Maupassant.

In 1882, Henry James met Turgenev here. About 50 years after this meeting of the great novelists, two beloved entertainers held a memorable evening: Maurice Chevalier remembers asking Josephine Baker to sing *J'ai deux amours* with him here.

## 2  Place de l'Opéra 9e

When Scott and Zelda Fitzgerald arrived in Paris in 1924 they moved into the Hôtel des Deux Mondes, at No. 22 Avenue de l'Opéra, before heading for the Riviera. Unaccustomed to French ways, they bathed Scottie in the bidet, which they mistook for a baby's bathtub. In Fitzgerald's 'Babylon Revisited', Charlie Wales takes a taxi ride down the Avenue de l'Opéra because

> he wanted to see the blue hour spread over the magnificent facade, and imagine that the cab horns, playing endlessly the first few bars of *Le Plus que Lent*, were the trumpets of the Second Empire. They were closing the iron grill in front of Brentano's bookstore and people were already at dinner behind the trim little bourgeois hedge of Duval's.

Two blocks down the avenue and to the left was once the Caves Mura (now Aux Cloches de Villedieu, No. 19) in rue d'Antin, where Hemingway bought his whiskey. In a letter to Harold Loeb (29 December 1924), he instructs Loeb to buy two bottles, for 'you can get it at the best price at the Cave Mura'. According to Carlos Baker, Hemingway was here having a drink with Bill Bird when he blurted out the news that he and Hadley were divorcing. When Bird asked him why, Hemingway answered: 'Because I am a son of a bitch'.

Hemingway's bank and his 'permanent address' beginning in 1926 was Guaranty Trust Company (1 rue des Italiens), further up the Boulevard des Italiens. In *A Moveable Feast* he recalls depositing his gambling money here. The Consulate General of the United States was established in this building. The *Stars and Stripes*, newspaper of the American Expeditionary Forces, was published here, beginning 1918-19. By November of 1933

Café de la Paix, with the Opéra to the right, as they look today.
Cummings, Dos Passos, and Gilbert Seldes had 'long bibulous and
conversational dinners' here in 1923, when the streets were less
crowded.

both Hemingway and Fitzgerald moved their banking and address to the
Guaranty Trust branch at 4 Place de la Concorde.

In the Place de l'Opéra, across the street from the café in the Lancel
building, was the *Chicago Daily News* office, where Paul Scott Mowrer
was working when he met Hadley in 1926.

**3 Chicago Daily News:** 8 Place de l'Opéra (10 Boulevard des
Capucines)
9e

Directly opposite the Café de la Paix were the offices of the *Chicago Daily
News* (now gone). Two brothers from Illinois served as Paris correspondents
for the *Daily News*. First was Paul Scott Mowrer, who would marry
Hadley Hemingway in 1933. Second was his younger brother Edgar Ansel
Mowrer, who was pressed into service (thus finding a career) when Paul
was sent to the front during the First World War. The elder Mowrer
describes this office:

> My office was right across from the Café de la Paix, at the corner
> of the Place de l'Opéra, one floor up, with a private entrance on
> the Boulevard des Capucines. It was the best place in town from

which to watch the Mardi Gras crowds or the military parades or the annual May Day riots. No tourist could come to Paris without seeing our big sign.

Our premises were luxuriously fitted, like a club, with palms and Oriental rugs and leather armchairs. We had a reading table provided with stationery. Also, we cabled home without charge, to be printed, the names of all Chicagoans who signed our register.

Edgar Mowrer, the author of several books, was 'the most persistently engaging conversationalist I know', according to John Gunther. Gunther also called Mowrer 'the best educated American I ever met'.

The Anglo-American Press Association of Paris met nearby on Wednesdays for lunch. They were an illustrious group, considering the presence of Hemingway. The 15 to 20 members included the congenial Morrill Cody and William Bird. Cody would later work for the American Embassy and Bird would become **Hemingway's second publisher (map D)**. Earlier in the century, according to Booth Tarkington, who attended their meetings, they were called the Wednesday Club and met 'near the Gare St. Lazare'.

Around the corner from the former *Chicago Daily News* office, continue up Boulevard des Capucines a short way until you reach rue de la Chaussée-d'Antin on your left. Boulevard des Capucines is one of the many grand boulevards cut through the old Paris by Baron Haussmann in the nineteenth century.

## 4  Paris Times: 2 rue de la Chaussée-d'Antin                          9e

The *Paris Times* (1924–9) was located here on the corner. Vincent Sheean and Hillet Bernstein worked at the *Times*, which *Herald* readers claimed catered to the 'lobster palace Americans' on the Right Bank. This was the briefest and least influential of the papers.

Continue a few steps up rue de la Chaussée-d'Antin and take the first left (rue Meyerbeer) toward the side of the Opéra. At 1 rue Meyerbeer is Paramount Pictures, which made films of *A Farewell to Arms* (1932), with Gary Cooper playing the Hemingway role, and *Islands in the Stream* (1977), with George C. Scott playing the Hemingway alter ego.

The projecting wing of the Opéra was built for subscribers who could drive to this private entrance in their carriages. You are going to walk around the Opéra (Place Diaghilev) to rue Scribe, but first look right on the

Boulevard Haussmann, home of two of the largest department stores in Paris (Galeries Lafayette and Magasins du Printemps).

If you look right, the rue La Fayette runs into the Boulevard Haussmann. Several blocks up rue La Fayette is rue Lamartine where at No. 5 was the location of the *Paris Tribune*. Although there is nothing historical to see there now, the Paris Edition of the *Chicago Tribune* was the most important paper for Left Bank artistic life. *The Left Bank Revisited: Selections from the Paris Tribune 1917-1934* (edited by Hugh Ford) bears witness to this importance. The paper gave good coverage to Joyce, Stein, Hemingway, and other writers. In a 1924 column, Eugene Jolas called Hemingway 'one of the most genuinely epic talents of any youngster writing in English today'. The paper was home to reporters William Shirer, Eugene Jolas, Elliot Paul, James Thurber, George Seldes, Henry Miller, and Waverly Root. Among their numerous memoirs see Shirer's *20th Century Journey 1904-1930* and Seldes' *Witness to a Century*.

Take rue Scribe along the other side of the Opéra. The Emperor's Pavilion with its double ramp was built to allow the king to drive straight to the royal box in his carriage. The Pavilion is now a library and museum.

## 5 American Express: 11 rue Scribe 9e

This corner building still is the banking, postal, and meeting centre for Americans. Although legend has it that Fitzgerald often started his afternoon here by picking up a cheque from his publisher — while other American expatriates only collected their letters from home — the writer actually picked up his cheques and mail at the Guaranty Trust Bank nearby. From the American Express, visiting Americans often walked over to the Boulevard des Capucines and the Café de la Paix, where the Fitzgeralds ate oysters.

George Webber, in Thomas Wolfe's *The Web and the Rock*, frustrated by the daily news that there is no letter from his girlfriend, is dismayed by the swarm of chattering, small-town American tourists in the American Express, here on their 'trip to Yurup'.

Henry Miller in *Tropic of Cancer* speaks often of the American Express. During his first visit to Paris in 1928 it is 'Paris! Meaning the Café Sélect, the Dôme, the Flea Market, the American Express! Paris!' But in the destitute 'miserable days' of 1930 this connection to home only means disappointment. When he had 'no appointments, no invitations to dinner, no program, no dough', he would 'each morning take the dreary walk to the American Express, and each morning [receive] the inevitable answer from the clerk'.

Cross rue Auber and continue down rue Scribe. Halfway down you will see the Grand Hôtel (No. 2) on your left and Hôtel Scribe (No. 1) on your right.

## 6  Hôtel Scribe: 1 rue Scribe                                               9e

Hemingway visited the Hôtel Scribe, which was a temporary lodging for newsmen during and between two wars. It served as press headquarters for the Allied Forces and among the correspondents who lived, ate, worked, and sometimes slept at Hôtel Scribe was Mary Welsh, who later became Hemingway's fourth wife. John Dos Passos stayed here in October 1945 while he was working as a correspondent. Dos Passos wrote home to his wife, Katy, that 'Paris looks almost frighteningly unchanged' except for the poverty of the people.

The hard times that Dos Passos observed after the war were similar to the economic hardships in the early 1930s, when George Orwell described trying to get a job at the Hôtel Scribe. 'We went to the Hôtel Scribe and waited an hour on the pavements', he writes in his semi-autobiographical novel *Down and Out in Paris and London*. The narrator and his friend Boris, a Russian immigrant, are unsuccessful in getting a job here. Eventually the narrator finds a job at 'Hôtel X', as he calls Hôtel Lotti, 7 rue de Castiglione.

From the Hôtel Scribe, cross the street to the Grand Hôtel and walk through the lobby, which usually displays pictures of the history of the hotel and the café. You can see on the wall the pictures of the building of the métro in front of the Opéra in 1905. Walk around the lounge coffee shop and leave by the Capucines door. When you exit into the Boulevard des Capucines (at No. 12) you will see Le Trou dans le Mur site directly across the street.

## 7  Le Trou dans le Mur (Hole in the Wall bar):
23 Boulevard des Capucines                                                     2e

Across the street from the Grand Hôtel and the Café de la Paix was (until 1988) another Hemingway haunt, a narrow bar (now a paella restaurant) that Hemingway called 'a hangout for deserters and for dope peddlers during and after the first war' — presumably because a rear exit opened into the sewers of Paris. The narrow back room is covered with gilded mirrors to give the impression of more space. There is a story in Hotchner's *Papa Hemingway* that after the appearance of *The Sun Also Rises*, Harold Loeb, the model for the unattractive Robert Cohn, said he would kill Hemingway. Hemingway announced, so the story goes, that he would be in The Hole in the Wall, whose mirrors, presumably, would allow him to spot his would-be assassin and duck out the back.

The romantic reputation of this bar contrasts sharply with the quiet opulence of this quarter. Between the Opéra and the Madeleine and the Place de la Concorde are many of the luxury shops of Paris.

Walk back toward the Place de l'Opéra and turn right just a few steps (cross rue de la Paix) into the Avenue de l'Opéra. Number 49 is on the right.

**8  New York Herald:** 49 Avenue de l'Opéra                    2e

The advertising and business office of the *New York Herald* (1887–1940) was a few doors below the Place and the Café de la Paix. It also held a large reading room where, at the turn of the century, one could read more than 100 American newspapers and periodicals. Note the grand, one-storey-high wooden door, the marble entrance and tall lamps.

Many well-known journalists worked for the *Herald*, from Ned Calmer, Harold Stearns and Eric Hawkins to Art Buchwald. For a full story of the Herald read *Hawkins of the Paris Herald* or Al Laney's *Paris Herald: The Incredible Newspaper.* Laney says the 'young intellectuals' working for the *Herald* frequented the Deux-Magots, dropped into Sylvia Beach's bookshop, and 'considered themselves as part of the Literary Revolution'.

**The Champs-Elysées office (map G)** was its chief editorial office. The print shop was at 38 rue du Louvre until 1930, thereafter at 21 rue de Berri. After the Second World War, publication resumed and Paul Scott Mowrer was editor. After a merger in 1967, it became the *International Herald Tribune* (map G).

Continue down the avenue. If you want to visit Brentano's bookstore, where it has been operating for decades, cross the next street (rue Daunou) to No. 37. If not, at this intersection turn right into rue Daunou and you will see another famous bar on the left.

**9  Harry's New York Bar:** 5 rue Daunou                    2e

Harry's New York Bar, birthplace of the Bloody Mary and the Sidecar,

Harry's New York Bar, 5 rue Daunou, is the Ivy League watering hole and birthplace of the Bloody Mary. Hemingway often dropped in to visit with an old friend Harry MacElhone. (*Robert E. Gajdusek*)

has gathered many legends itself during the last 80 years. Here is where Hemingway went after boxing at the Montmartre Sportif. Harry MacElhone, the proprietor, served as the author's second, while his son, Andy, played with Jack (Bumby). Hemingway's photographs hang on the wall. Harry's is one of those places that is cosy with dark wood, where, as one visitor explained, 'drinks don't come with paper umbrellas and time passes slower over the edge of a glass'. It is a saloon in a city of cafés: 'Look out for those swingin' doors' is painted on the door. The 'Sank Roo Doe Noo' sign is probably an aid to taxi-taking monolingual American tourists. The bar has appeared in a hundred customers' novels from Hemingway to Sinclair Lewis's *Dodsworth* and Ian Fleming's James Bond novels.

A favourite haunt of Fitzgerald, this bar is a parody of the Ivy League style that nourished (and oppressed) him. College banners hang in the back, pictures of sports figures on the wall. Single women may not feel at home here.

When you leave Harry's New York Bar, turn left to rue de la Paix and turn left again. Walk down rue de la Paix, past Cartier and other elegant jewellery shops, to the Place Vendôme, with its seventeenth-century architecture. The column, ahead, was placed there by Napoleon in 1810. Enter the Ritz Hotel from the Place Vendôme (No. 15) only if you are very well-dressed and look like you may be living there. Otherwise turn right into rue des Capucines, then left into rue Cambon.

## 10  Hemingway's Bar at the Ritz Hotel: 38 rue Cambon      le

Perhaps the most famous and most expensive Hemingway haunt is the Ritz in the Place Vendôme. It was built in 1705 as a private mansion by Jules Hardouin-Mansard and opened as a hotel in 1898 by César Ritz, with Escoffier in the kitchen. The Ritz is synonymous with elegance, and the doorman guards its reputation. A trip to the rue Cambon bar may get you in the door. There is also a lovely garden restaurant at this entrance to the hotel. Just inside the rue Cambon entrance to the hotel is the Hemingway bar, formerly the ladies' bar during segregated days, to the right, and the regular Espadon bar to the left.

Long before Hemingway could afford to, King Vidor, the Hollywood producer, gave great parties here. He and Fitzgerald had met on a ship to France in 1928. The Ritz, according to newspaperman William Shirer, was 'full of Ivy Leaguers who had gone into business or banking, and apparently it was compatible for a Princeton graduate such as Scott', who 'preferred it to the cafés of Montparnasse'. A drunken Fitzgerald had to be helped into taxis to get home from the parties. The best writing about the Ritz bar is in his *Tender is the Night* and 'Babylon Revisited'.

Hemingway's bar at the rue Cambon side of the Ritz Hotel was formerly the smaller 'ladies' bar' before women were allowed to drink with the men. Charles Ritz wanted to honour one of his most famous guests.

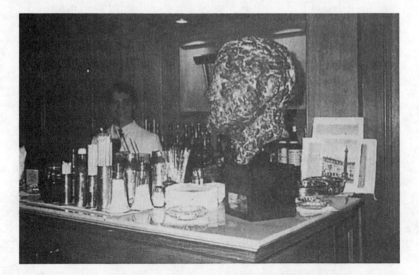

In *Tender is the Night*, he captures the elegant details of the hotel as well as the leisure of his expatriate characters:

Abe North was still in the Ritz bar, where he had been since nine in the morning. When he arrived seeking sanctuary the windows were open and great beams were busy at pulling up the dust from smoky carpets and cushions. Chasseurs tore through the corridors, liberated and disembodied, moving for the moment in pure space . . .

The famous Paul, the concessionnaire, had not arrived, but Claude, who was checking stock, broke off his work with no improper surprise to make Abe a pick-me-up. Abe sat on a bench against a wall. After two drinks he began to feel better — so much better that he mounted to the barber's shop and was shaved. When he returned to the bar Paul had arrived . . . Paul liked Abe and came over to talk.

'I was supposed to ship home this morning,' Abe said, 'I mean yesterday morning, or whatever this is.'

'Why din you?' asked Paul.

Abe considered, and happened finally to reason: 'I was reading a serial in Liberty and the next installment was due here in Paris — so if I'd sailed I'd have missed it — then I never would have read it.'

In a story entitled 'The Bridal Party', Fitzgerald sets a bachelor dinner in the Ritz. Unlike his passage in *Tender is the Night*, which creates a sense of the place itself, Fitzgerald here evokes only the frenzy of activity:

The Ritz Bar had been prepared for the occasion by French and American banners and by a great canvas covering one wall, against which the guests were invited to concentrate their proclivities in breaking glasses.

At the first cocktail, taken at the bar, there were many slight spillings from many trembling hands, but later, with the champagne, there was a rising tide of laughter and occasional bursts of song.

In another of his short stories, 'News of Paris — Fifteen Years Ago', Henry Dell (the protagonist) attends a wedding reception at the Ritz. Like the character in 'The Bridal Party', Henry had once been the lover of the bride. 'When the confusion and din were at their height, he went out into the rue Cambon' to escape in a taxi.

After the Crash, most high-spending Americans had deserted the bar and Paris. The American Charlie Wales in Fitzgerald's 'Babylon Revisited' returns to Paris in 1930 to find great changes in his old haunts, chief among them the Ritz bar:

> He was not really disappointed to find Paris was so empty. But the stillness in the Ritz bar was strange and portentous. It was not an American bar any more — he felt polite in it, and not as if he owned it. It had gone back into France. He felt the stillness from the moment he got out of the taxi and saw the doorman, usually in a frenzy of activity at this hour, gossiping with the *chasseur* by the servants' entrance.

Later in the story Paul the bartender tells him sadly, 'we do about half the business we did. So many fellows I hear about back in the States lost everything, maybe not in the first crash, but then in the second.' Such frequent fictional use of this bar would suggest that Fitzgerald was a regular here, though later Hemingway would claim that the bartender at the Ritz said he did not remember who Fitzgerald was.

Hemingway led a band of dusty soldiers into the lobby of the Ritz in 1944 and ordered 73 dry martinis; later Marlene Dietrich sat on the edge of the bathtub and sang as Ernest shaved in his room here. In the hotel he asked Mary Welsh to be his fourth wife. Among those who visited him here after the Liberation were Sergeant J. D. Salinger, Jean-Paul Sartre, Simone de Beauvoir, Orson Welles, and George Orwell. Simone de Beauvoir remembers that when she visited Hemingway immediately after the Liberation, he was ill with the flu and lying in his pyjamas on one of the two beds with brass headboards. There were several half-empty bottles of Scotch on a table 'within easy reach'. Hemingway 'heaved himself up' and hugged Sartre, calling him a 'general' — adding, 'me I'm only a captain'. Sartre corrected him, and they all sat down for a night of drinking and conversation. Sartre left sleepily at three in the morning, Beauvoir 'stayed until dawn'.

Grateful for his famous presence, the Ritz renamed its smaller rue Cambon bar the Hemingway Bar. There is no evidence that Hemingway left notebooks in any trunk in the basement of the Ritz, as myth has it.

When you exit the Hemingway Bar into rue Cambon, glance right across the street to where the *Brooklyn Daily Eagle* was once located at No. 53 on the corner. Guy Hickok, probably Hemingway's best friend among the foreign correspondents, worked for the *Eagle*. Hemingway visited him there and benefited from his press pass to sporting events. Turn left and walk down rue Cambon. William Bird lived for a while at No. 39, and Coco Chanel reigned over fashion for half a century at No. 31. On the third floor of No. 29, Henry James lived from 1875 to 1876, when he was writing *The American*. Hemingway admired James's fiction, especially his dialogue, and once half jokingly wrote to Hadley that he could possibly 'turn out to be the Henry James of the People'.

Unless you want to visit Hôtel Saint-James and Albany, skip the next entry; the original building, once located several blocks to the left, is no longer there. Instead turn right. When you see the church of Notre-Dame de l'Assomption, called the Polish church, turn right for a few steps into rue Duphot to find No. 12.

## 11 'This Quarter' printer: 338 rue Saint-Honoré le

Here (the site is now a building, a garage/office) was the printer of books and magazines, the Imprimerie de Herbert Clark. During the late winter and early spring of 1925 Hemingway spent many hours here helping Ernest Walsh with the first number of his *This Quarter*, which included Hemingway's 'Big Two-Hearted River'. Walsh was an itinerant poet, originally from Michigan, who was suffering from tuberculosis. Because the first issue of the magazine was dedicated to Ezra Pound, Hemingway asked Man Ray for a photograph of Pound. After *The Dial* turned down his short story 'The Undefeated' because it was too frank, Hemingway sold it to Walsh for the second issue of *This Quarter*. Hemingway's chapter on Ernest Walsh in *A Moveable Feast* is entitled 'The Man Who Was Marked for Death'. Walsh died in 1926.

At 211 rue Saint-Honoré (Hôtel Saint-James and Albany) Sinclair Lewis and his family lived in October 1921. Lewis was working on *Babbitt* at the time. Five months before, the Fitzgeralds stayed here briefly on their first European excursion. Typically, they disrupted hotel service, melting ice cream on the windowsill and tying the elevator open so it would be available. They stood for an hour outside the home of Anatole France, hoping to see the great French writer (who won the Nobel Prize that year), but Fitzgerald concluded superficially that the country 'is a bore and a disappointment, chiefly, I imagine, because we know no one here'.

Walk up rue Saint-Honoré. Beside the entrance to the church, turn right and walk a few steps into rue Duphot.

## 12  Prunier Restaurant: 9 rue Duphot                    1e

Here is a favourite sea-food restaurant of Hemingway and Fitzgerald near the Place de la Madeleine. Prunier (there is a second one at 16 Avenue Victor Hugo) was founded in 1872 (the washroom is a historical monument!) and was a mecca for Paris gourmets. Emile Prunier planted beds of Cape Cod clams and Blue Point oysters and took out generous advertising space in the *Paris Herald*, which paid off well in the American expatriate community. In Thomas Wolfe's *Of Time and the River*, Eugene Gant and his friends eat here often.

Hemingway was an occasional customer over 30 years. He and Fitzgerald dined here before the fateful boxing match between Hemingway and Callaghan. Fitzgerald forgot to call time at two minutes, and when Hemingway landed on the floor, Fitzgerald burst out with 'Oh, my God! I let the round go four minutes'. Hemingway did not forgive him.

In *A Moveable Feast* Hemingway describes a successful day at the races for Hadley and him in the 1920s:

we stopped at Pruniers on the way home, going in to sit at the bar

Prunier's was the favourite sea-food restaurant of American expatriates. Hemingway and Fitzgerald dined together here before a boxing match between Hemingway and Callaghan.

after looking at all the clearly priced wonders in the window. We had oysters and *crabe Mexicaine* with glasses of Sancerre. We walked back through the Tuileries in the dark.

Mary Hemingway remembers that after the Second World War they ate with Marlene Dietrich here and drank two bottles of Sancerre.

The Fitzgeralds ate here in the spring of 1925 when they lived nearby in the Hôtel Florida (Boulevard Malesherbes), when their **apartment near the Arc de Triomphe** was being renovated for their occupancy **(map G)**. They usually preferred the Pouilly and bouillabaisse.

Further up rue Duphot and around the corner to the right is the Boulevard de la Madeleine, a street often walked by Hemingway, but probably not worth the detour. His description, however, is worth reading.

## 13 Boulevard de la Madeleine                                    le

In a sentence written in 1922 (and not included in any of his books), Hemingway presents a dramatic sequence of simple details that he has witnessed:

> I have seen the one legged street walker who works in the Boulevard Madeleine between the Rue Cambon and Bernheim-Jeune's limping along the pavement through the crowd on a rainy night with a beefy red-faced Episcopal clergyman holding an umbrella over her.

Hemingway presents the details of a drama, leaving the reader to interpret the relationship. He does not make any value judgements, nor does he say how the scene affected him. He is only the observer and recorder of the scene.

It is worth pointing out that it was at the art dealer Bernheim-Jeune that Hemingway saw a number of paintings of Paul Cézanne in the 1920s.

Return back down rue Duphot and across the front of the Polish church and right into rue Cambon, which will take you to the Tuileries Gardens. You will see the gates ahead. This is the route from Prunier Restaurant that Hemingway describes in the passage from *A Moveable Feast* that follows.

## 14 Tuileries Gardens                                            le

As you cross rue de Rivoli to enter the gardens, the Place de la Concorde is to your right and the Louvre to your left through the gardens. The Hemingways turned left at the fountain:

> We walked back through the Tuileries in the dark and stood and looked through the Arc du Carrousel up across the dark gardens with the lights of the Concorde behind the formal darkness and then the long rise of lights toward the Arc de Triomphe. Then we looked back toward the dark of the Louvre and I said, 'Do you really think that the three arches are in line?'

If you try the same vista, not as Hemingway did but from the fountain, you now see two changes: Pei's glass pyramid behind the left side of the Arc du Carrousel and, in the other direction, La Défense skyscrapers crowding the view of the Arc de Triomphe.

Although Ernest and Hadley walked through the gateway of the Louvre and across the bridge of the Seine toward their home on the Left Bank, you may wish to visit other Hemingway sites on the Right Bank, starting at the Place de la Concorde.

Numerous references in other American fiction describe walking in the Place de la Concorde and the Tuileries — from Henry James's *The Ambassadors*, where 'a soft breeze and sprinkled smell' flit in the light to Henry Miller's *Tropic of Cancer*, where he describes walking in the garden and 'getting an erection looking at the dumb statues'.

In Fitzgerald's *Tender is the Night*, Dick Diver and Rosemary ride through Place de la Concorde. In a style quite different from the frankness of Miller or the bare realism of Hemingway, Fitzgerald captures the romance of this scene:

> and lovers now they fell ravenously on the quick seconds while outside the taxi windows the green and cream twilight faded, and the fire-red, gas-blue, ghost-green signs begin to shine smokily through the tranquil rain. It was nearly six, the streets were in movement, the bistros gleamed, the Place de la Concorde moved by in pink majesty as the cab turned north.

# 8

# HEMINGWAY AND FITZGERALD OFF THE CHAMPS-ELYSEES

Hem was mad about bicycle racing. He used to get himself up in a striped jumper like a contestant on the Tour de France and ride around the exterior boulevards with his knees up to his ears and his chin between the handlebars. It seemed silly to me but in those days Hem submitted to a certain amount of kidding.

John Dos Passos, who could not ride a bicycle

On emerging from the métro stop at the Place de la Concorde in 1916, Ezra Pound was struck by the visual impression of beautiful faces and, after 18 months of rewriting and distilling its poetic expression, penned his famous Imagist poem entitled 'In the Station of the Metro':

The apparition of these faces in the crowd;
Petals on a wet, black bough.

The magnificent Place has undoubtedly been an inspiration for other poets, as it was for Pound and for Fitzgerald, who wrote, 'One thing is certain — that before you melt out into the green-and-cream Paris twilight you will have the feeling of standing for a moment at one of the predestined centers of the world'.

Hemingway, whose small output of poetry was largely uninspired, came frequently to the Hôtel de Crillon, which faces the Place. He did not live in the area that is covered on this map, but he made important visits here, not just to the Crillon bar, which he mentions in several works, but to newspaper offices, to the apartment of Pauline and the church nearby where they were married, to the American Hospital in Neuilly for stitches in his head, and to the apartments of the Murphys and the Fitzgeralds.

To live in the 8th and 16th arrondissements was expensive living. It is more appropriately the territory of the Fitzgeralds: they lived in at least three apartments here. The Murphys introduced the Fitzgeralds to the

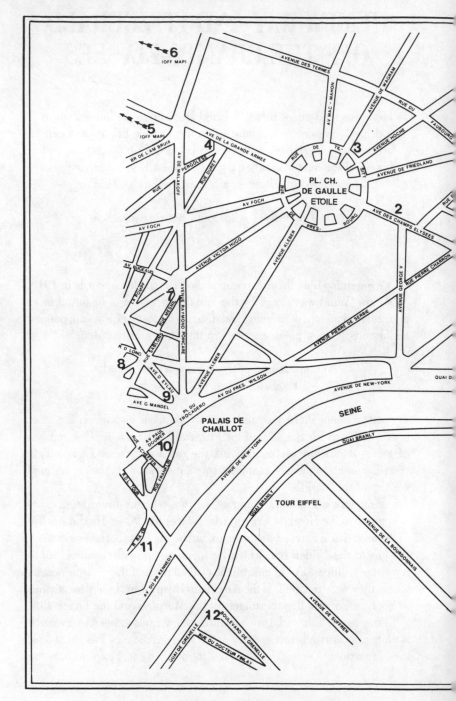

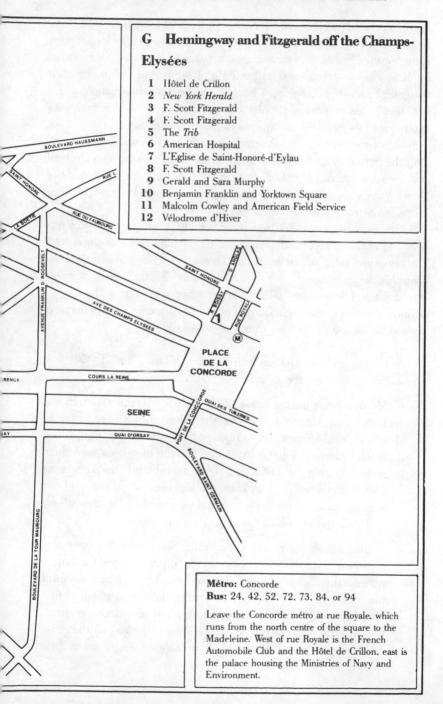

**G   Hemingway and Fitzgerald off the Champs-Elysées**

1   Hôtel de Crillon
2   *New York Herald*
3   F. Scott Fitzgerald
4   F. Scott Fitzgerald
5   The *Trib*
6   American Hospital
7   L'Eglise de Saint-Honoré-d'Eylau
8   F. Scott Fitzgerald
9   Gerald and Sara Murphy
10   Benjamin Franklin and Yorktown Square
11   Malcolm Cowley and American Field Service
12   Vélodrome d'Hiver

PLACE
DE LA
CONCORDE

SEINE

**Métro:** Concorde
**Bus:** 24, 42, 52, 72, 73, 84, or 94

Leave the Concorde métro at rue Royale, which
runs from the north centre of the square to the
Madeleine. West of rue Royale is the French
Automobile Club and the Hôtel de Crillon, east is
the palace housing the Ministries of Navy and
Environment.

Parisian art and music world. Neither couple spent long periods in Paris. Fitzgerald's visits are measured in months — interrupted by longer stays in the South of France or in sanatoriums in Switzerland. During their months in Paris, Zelda worked hard on her ballet lessons and on rearing their daughter Scottie to be a flapper ('because flappers are brave and gay and beautiful'). Scott worked fitfully on his writings, and their health deteriorated — his from alcohol, hers from mental illness.

Some of the locations on this map are within easy walking distance. Only the intrepid will want to take buses to the outlying American Hospital and the *International Herald Tribune* in Neuilly. Only the afficionado of Hemingway's sports fetishes will want to journey beyond this map to seek his favourite racecourses and arenas.

Hemingway spent as much time watching and participating in athletics as he did working. He boxed, played tennis, and attended sporting events. The site of one arena where he attended boxing matches and bicycle races is on this map, though the arena itself (see Site No. 12) was torn down 30 years ago. The scenes of all the other sporting events are in the remote arrondissements of the Right Bank. Four of his favourite arenas (located beyond the scope of this map) are the following:

1      Cirque d'Hiver, 110 rue Amelot (11e). Métro: Filles-du-Calvaire. Scene of 'great twenty-round fights'.

2      Ménilmontant boxing arena (20e). Métro: Ménilmontant. Sylvia Beach tells an amusing story of when she and Adrienne Monnier accompanied Ernest and a pregnant Hadley to the boxing matches at the Pelleport Club. He explained that the blood was 'only their noses'. During the last fight, she remembered, the spectators participated: 'with the socking, the kicking, the yelling, and the surging back and forth, I was afraid we would be "hemmed" in, and that Hadley would be injured in the melee'.

3      Enghien-les-Bains racecourse: Train: Soisy-Saint-Montmorency (from the Gare du Nord). Hemingway often attended the horse-races at this 'beautiful track'. He and Hadley went by train from the Gare du Nord through the slums to the racecourse that Hemingway described as: 'the small, pretty and larcenous track that was the home of the outsider'. They picnicked on the grass near the grandstand. Half of their winnings were placed in their betting pot.

4      Hippodrome d'Auteuil, Bois de Boulogne. Métro: Porte d'Auteuil. The Grand Steeplechase is 'a damned fine race', he wrote to Maxwell Perkins, his editor. 'I worked two tracks in their season when I could, Auteuil and Enghien . . . I finally stopped because it took too much time.' Decades later he boasted to A. E. Hotchner of his inside information: 'I was the only outsider who was allowed into the private training grounds at Achères, outside of Maisons-Lafitte, and Chantilly'.

John Dos Passos remembers that Hemingway was also 'mad' about bicycle racing and, in a 'striped jumper like a contestant on the Tour de France', would 'ride around the exterior boulevards with his knees up to his ears and his chin between the handlebars.' In sports, Hemingway found many metaphors, such as the 'fixed race', for his fiction and life.

Although these racecourses and arenas are distant, one can find the major Right Bank haunts (west of Place de la Concorde) that Hemingway and Fitzgerald frequented. This territory is also rich in Franco-American history.

**1  Hôtel de Crillon:** 10 Place de la Concorde           8e

The famous old Hôtel de Crillon was built facing the Place de la Concorde in 1775. 'When I had money', admits Hemingway, 'I went to the Crillon'. In *The Sun Also Rises*, Jake waits for Brett, who stands him up at the Crillon. At first he waits in the library (now a shop), just inside the front door to the left:

> At five o'clock I was in the Hotel Crillon waiting for Brett. She was not there, so I sat down and wrote some letters. They were not good letters but I hoped their being on Crillon stationery would help them. Brett did not turn up, so about quarter to six I went down to the bar and had a Jack Rose with George the barman.

Later in the novel Bill drops in at the Crillon bar:

> Stopped at the Crillon. George made me a couple of Jack Roses. George's a great man. Know the secret of his success? Never been daunted.
> 'You'll be daunted after about three more pernods.'
> 'Not in public. If I begin to feel daunted I'll go off by myself.'

The Hôtel de Crillon is to the far left of the Place de la Concorde in
this picture, taken a decade before Hemingway arrived in Paris. 'Oné
of the predestined centers of the world', Fitzgerald calls this square.

The Crillon bar was assumed to be the longest in Europe and was a favourite
spot of both Hemingway and Fitzgerald. Built in 1907, it was removed
about four years ago and the room became the restaurant l'Obélisque,
with an entrance on rue Boissy d'Anglas.

The dying Harry and his wife talk of the Crillon in Hemingway's 'The
Snows of Kilimanjaro':

> 'Where did we stay in Paris?' he asked the woman who was sitting
> by him in a canvas chair, now, in Africa.
> 'At the Crillon. You know that.'
> 'Why do I know that?'
> 'That's where we always stayed.'

In 1978 I found one of the few surviving members of the American
expatriate community of the 1920s living at the Crillon. Florence Gilliam,
co-editor of the first little magazine (*Gargoyle*) of this community, lived

her final years in this majestic old hotel.

The Crillon is both a popular place for social rendezvous as well as an important historical setting. On behalf of the 13 independent colonies, Benjamin Franklin signed here the Treaty of Friendship and Trade with Louis XVI. In 1919, the commission responsible for drafting the League of Nations covenant stayed at the Crillon. The first agreement was signed in the hotel's Salon des Aigles. At the end of the Second World War, some of the worse fighting occurred on the steps of the Crillon, which later served as Supreme Headquarters for the Allied Expeditionary Force. The American Embassy is next-door (on your right as you leave the hotel) at 2 Avenue Gabriel.

Many British and American writers set their scenes at the Crillon. Edith Wharton's *A Son at the Front*, set in wartime Paris, opens at the Crillon. In Dos Passos' *Nineteen-Nineteen*, when Dick Savage comes to Paris for the Peace Conference, 'the hub of Paris was the Hôtel de Crillon, its artery the rue Royale'. In Noel Coward's *Hay Fever*, novelist David Blios 'got it all muddled' in the Crillon.

The Crillon faces the Chamber of Deputies and the Quai d'Orsay across the Seine. To the left around the corner from the Crillon in rue Royale is Maxim's restaurant, and across from Maxim's at No. 6 lived Madame de Staël at the end of the eighteenth century. To the right as you leave the hotel, and a short walk up the Avenue Gabriel (past the American Embassy), is the Palais de l'Elysée, the residence of the President of the French Republic.

The Place de la Concorde received its placid name after blood-soaked years (1793–5) here when the guillotine cut the neck of Louis XVI, Marie-Antoinette, Mme du Barry, Danton, Robespierre, and nearly 1400 others. The obelisk was erected in 1836. Less than a century later Zelda and Scott Fitzgerald, so legend has it, entertained themselves by frivolously racing around the obelisk in a stolen delivery-cart tricycle. He used the incident, placing it at the Etoile, in 'Babylon Revisited'.

No other point gives such a sweep of the grand spaces of Paris. Beside the slow curve of the Seine are the two tree-lined prospects: the wide view right down Champs-Elysées to the Arc de Triomphe, and left the smaller tree-lined walk of the Tuileries with the smaller Arc and the pyramid beyond. Henry James's Nick Dormer, in the fifth chapter of *The Tragic Muse* (1890), stands at the edge of this 'great square' and looks out over the 'bank of the Seine, the steep blue roofs of the quay, the bright immensity of Paris'.

The Avenue des Champs-Elysées begins at the Place de la Concorde. Take a 73 bus in front of the Hôtel de Crillon and ride up Champs-Elysées. You may ride all the way up the avenue or stop at Avenue George V near the Lido, where at No. 120 the *New York Herald* was once located and across the street is the historic Fouquet's restaurant (No. 99).

As you walk or ride up the avenue, notice that it seems to divide itself into three parts: the long garden area (with embassies, theatres, the president's palace, and grand museums off through the trees); the Rond-Point intersected by four streets; and the commercial, overbuilt avenue that gently climbs to the Etoile and the Arc de Triomphe. Thomas Jefferson, then Ambassador from the United States, lived from 1785 to 1789 at No. 92 (on the right at the corner of 2 rue de Berri). Vanderbilt lived at No. 138, Baron Rothschild at No. 140.

Janet Flanner, Hemingway's journalist buddy, describes the change in Champs-Elysées as occurring just before the early 1930s when it 'suddenly burst out with a rash of colored cinema signs' from the ground floor of the mansions. At the top of the avenue, 12 avenues intersect to form l'Etoile (the star), now called Place Charles-de-Gaulle; the streets are named to commemorate Napoleon's victories. On the street a block before the intersection, on rue de Tilsitt, is one of the homes of the Fitzgeralds (No. 3).

According to William Faulkner, in August of 1925, he walked

> through the Bois de Boulogne, up the avenue to the Place de l'Etoile, where the Arc de Triomphe is. I sat there a while watching the expensive foreign cars full of American movie actresses whizzing past, then I walked down the Champs-Elysées to the Place de Concorde, and had lunch . . . at a restaurant where cabmen and janitors eat.

Unlike the Fitzgeralds, Faulkner was more comfortable with the working class.

## 2 New York Herald (Paris): 120 Avenue des Champs-Elysées 8e

An expatriate's umbilical cord to his mother country began four generations ago when James Gordon Bennett Jr — who sent Henry Morton Stanley to find Dr David Livingstone in Africa — founded a Paris edition of the *New York Herald*. He founded the Paris edition on 4 October 1887 and used this townhouse for his head editorial office.

The flamboyant Bennett had been living grandly on the Avenue des Champs-Elysées, lunching daily at the Tour d'Argent, and running his *Herald* in New York City via telegraph. In order to have a news-staff he could more easily dominate, he founded his European edition. Bennett introduced the linotype, half-tone engravings, and comic strips to Europe. He also ran up a $100,000-a-year loss. He ruled with an iron hand and whim, but he never missed an issue during the First World War, when the *Herald* was the only paper of any language published in Paris.

Bennett died before the Allied victory, when the presence of the American Army increased sales from 12,000 to 100,000 copies. In 1920, Frank Munsey purchased the *Paris Herald*, the *New York Telegram*, and the impoverished (5000 circulation) *New York Herald*. In 1924, Munsey sold the *Herald* papers to Ogden Reid, son of Whitelaw Reid of the *New York Tribune*, who merged the two New York papers (see **map F**).

During the 1920s, Paris newspapers and newsmen were lively. The *Herald* and its rivals — the *Paris Times*, the Paris edition of the *Chicago Tribune*, and the continental edition of the *Daily Mail* of London — employed many talented writers who hoped to write the 'great American novel' or were publishing avant-garde magazines and running hand presses for limited editions.

The Depression killed all English-language newspapers except the *Herald*, which suspended only when the German forces invaded Paris. 'Great Battle for Paris at Crucial Stage' read its last headline on 12 June 1940. After the Second World War, the *Herald* took over the offices vacated by *Stars and Stripes*, the servicemen's newspaper. This office is located two blocks down the Champs-Elysées in rue de Berri. The Ogden Reid family sold both the *New York Herald* and its Paris edition to John Hay Whitney. The *Washington Post* bought half his interest in the *Paris Herald* when the New York paper closed. In 1967 the major competition, 'Punch' Sulzberger's international edition of the *New York Times*, joined the *Paris Herald*. It was rechristened the *International Herald Tribune* and moved west to the other side of the Arc de Triomphe (see Site No. 5).

In a centenary volume commemorating the paper in 1987, Art Buchwald, long since returned to journalism in the United States, recalls the old offices at 21 rue de Berri, where he spent what he calls 'magical days and nights . . . in that rickety building'. He gets 'misty-eyed' at the recollection, feeling about it 'the way General MacArthur felt about West Point': 'it's the place where we were born again'.

Continue up the avenue to the outer ring that circles the arch, and turn right into rue de Tilsitt, one block before the circle. The Fitzgerald site is at the corner of Avenue de Wagram.

## 3  F. Scott Fitzgerald: 14 rue de Tilsitt                                   8e

Zelda and Scott Fitzgerald lived here a block from the side of the Arc de Triomphe in the spring of 1925, when Scott was not yet 29 years old. The Fitzgerald apartment (a fifth-floor walk-up) had a lovely address at the east corner of Avenue de Wagram, yet it was decorated in what one friend called 'early Galeries Lafayette'. Scott was at the height of his fame but in debt to Scribner's. *The Great Gatsby* was a critical success, but sales never covered his expenses. In the autumn of that year, Fitzgerald wrote to H. L. Mencken that he had 'met most of the American literary world here (the crowd that centres about Pound) and find them mostly junk-dealers; except a few like Hemingway who are doing rather more thinking and working'.

The Hemingways had lunch here with the Fitzgeralds after the men met at the **Dingo** (see **Site No. 13, map E**) in April 1925. Hemingway describes the lunch in this flat in *A Moveable Feast*. He remembered the flat as 'gloomy and airless', with nothing of their personal possessions in it.

> I cannot remember much about the flat except that it was gloomy and airless and that there was nothing in it that seemed to belong to them except Scott's first books bound in light blue leather with the titles in gold. Scott also showed us a large ledger with all of the stories he had published listed in it year after year with the prices he had received for them and also the amounts received for any motion picture sales, and the sales and royalties of his books. They were all noted as carefully as the log of a ship and Scott showed them to both of us with impersonal pride as though he were the curator of a museum. Scott was nervous and hospitable and he showed us his accounts of his earnings as though they had been the view. There was no view.

Fitzgerald was dismayed that Hemingway and Zelda took an immediate dislike to each other: she thought Hemingway was 'bogus', and he thought she was a jealous and predatory wife. The friendship of the two men was finally strained beyond recovery during a 1929 trip to Paris by Fitzgerald, when Hemingway tried to avoid him, and Pauline let her disapproval of the Fitzgeralds be known.

Scott, Zelda, and Scottie Fitzgerald high-stepping their Christmas
greeting of 1925 in their rue de Tilsitt apartment. Zelda brought the
Christmas decorations from home. (*Princeton University Library*)

During this 1925 residency, according to his French biographer, André
Le Vot, Fitzgerald was feeling 'at home in Paris now and highly critical
of unenterprising American tourists'. Yet others remember that he was
drunk for days and weeks on end. William Shirer recalls that Fitzgerald
would turn up staggering drunk in the offices of the *Chicago Tribune* on

**rue Lamartine (see No. 4, map F),** shouting that he wanted to help them get the 'goddam paper' to press. Shirer describes one of the several times that he and James Thurber and Eugene Jolas took Fitzgerald home in a taxi to rue de Tilsitt:

> The apartment house stood back behind an iron grille fence and from an upper story a woman appeared at a window and shouted, 'Scott, you bastard! You're drunk again!'
>
> 'Zelda, darling . . . Yuh . . . Yuh . . . re . . . wrong . . . dead wrong . . . I . . . I'm sober, darling . . . really . . . I am . . . as . . . as . . . a . . . polar bear.' He sort of sang out the words as best he could . . .
>
> With two of us hauling away at his arms and the other two pushing we tried to lug the famous writer through the gate. No go. He broke away. Now he was furious as only a frustrated drunk could be. Circling around behind us he ran to the curb and picked up a piece of iron grating from around the trunk of a tree. He was about to bash in Thurber's head from behind when Jolas jumped on him and brought him down . . . Finally, we just carried him in, while Zelda, in pajamas, welcomed him with curses, and then, suddenly changing her mood, insisted that we stay and have a drink, which we mercifully declined.

It was a 'terrible winter', according to Zelda, because the flat could not be ventilated and 'smelled of a church chancery'. The Fitzgeralds left France in March of 1926. In 1928 (April–August), after they had discovered the Left Bank, they lived across from the Luxembourg Gardens at 58 rue de Vaugirard, at the corner of **rue Bonaparte (map B).**

Return to the Etoile Charles-de-Gaulle on Avenue de Wagram. E. E. Cummings describes an altercation here between the police (flics) and communist demonstrators in the mid-1920s. In his poem '16 heures/l'Etoile', Cummings says that the communists were outnumbered fifty to one when —

> . . . the flics rush
> batter the crowd sprawls collapses
> singing knocked down trampled the kicked by
> flics rush . . .

You should skip the next three locations, which take you quite a distance west and, with the exception of the hospital, have nothing to show you. Therefore, if you wish to go directly to the church where Pauline Pfeiffer and Ernest Hemingway were married (No. 7), walk (or take a No. 52 bus) on the opposite side of the Etoile from Wagram and the Fitzgerald home. Walk right around the circle to Avenue Victor-Hugo. Get off the bus in the Place Victor-Hugo.

If you are intrepid and insist on visiting the next three locations, you can walk to rue Pergolèse (or take a No. 73 bus for one stop). The 73 bus will also take you to the *Trib.* On the way you pass No. 36, where in a fifth-floor room in 1927 Stephen Vincent Benet worked on 'John Brown's Body'. Then a No. 82 bus at Place de la Porte Maillot will take you to the hospital.

## 4  F. Scott Fitzgerald: 10 rue Pergolèse                          16e

The Fitzgeralds moved here in the autumn of 1929 after returning from the South of France and spending a few days in a hotel in rue du Bac on the Left Bank. He worked on *Tender is the Night* here. Pergolèse runs from Avenue de la Grande-Armée (at the Place du Général-Patton) to Avenue Foch and is just a short walk from the Bois de Boulogne.

Fitzgerald encouraged his literary agent, Harold Ober, to pass on to Hemingway any work or film offers for the latter's novels, without using Fitzgerald's name: 'you see my relations with him are entirely friendly and not business and he'd merely lose confidence in me if he felt he was being hemmed in by any coalition'. Hemingway did encourage Fitzgerald's intervention when a negative story surfaced in New York about his boxing match with Morley Callaghan. Though Callaghan challenged the story (that he had knocked out Hemingway) before Fitzgerald could give the correct version, Fitzgerald was nevertheless caught in the middle of the crossfire between Hemingway and Callaghan. He did write to warn his editor, Max Perkins, against the 'lies' of Robert McAlmon, 'a bitter rat' who gossiped about both Fitzgerald and Hemingway.

Zelda continued her ballet lessons, yet ignored an invitation from the San Carlo Opera Ballet Company in Naples to dance a solo role in *Aida*. Her periods of withdrawal and mental illness increased. On 23 April 1930 Zelda entered a hospital called Malmaison on the outskirts of Paris, but left on 2 May.

**5 The Trib:** 181 avenue Charles-de-Gaulle                    Neuilly

Today, beyond the Place de la Porte-Maillot, almost in the shadow of La
Defénse (a high-rise concrete business centre), copy for the *International
Herald Tribune* (called the 'Trib') originates in this bland nine-storey
building. The 40 or more editors use material from a couple of full-time
reporters, numerous associated columnists, and news columns from
correspondents of the *New York Times*, the *Los Angeles Times*, and the
*Washington Post*. Today the paper has over 300,000 readers and appears
in simultaneous facsimiled editions in other cities such as London, Zurich,
and Tokyo.

**6 American Hospital:** 63 Boulevard Victor-Hugo                    Neuilly

North of Avenue Charles-de-Gaulle off Boulevard du Château in Neuilly
— just a block from the Seine — is the American Hospital. In June of
1926 Zelda Fitzgerald had her appendix removed here after suffering
from colitis. She recovered and returned to the Riviera.

In the middle of one night in March 1928, Archibald MacLeish and
Pauline Hemingway rushed the accident-prone Ernest by cab to this hospital
(entrance formerly at 44 rue Chauveau). The doctor took nine stitches
to close the gash above his right eye made by a falling skylight in the
bathroom at his rue Férou apartment. He had pulled the wrong cord.
(Hemingway later told A. E. Hotchner that the doctor was the Carl Weiss
who later shot Huey Long.) MacLeish, who had been called by Pauline
to help, thought that Hemingway was drunk. The press picked up the
incident and Pound wrote from Italy to ask 'How the hellsuffering tomcats'
could Hemingway 'git drunk enough to fall upwards thru the blithering
skylight!!!!!!!'

After suffering from digestive problems and fatigue, Gertrude Stein was
taken to the American Hospital 19 July 1956. Eight days later, after
enduring great pain and at her insistence, doctors operated on her abdomen.
The tumour was cancerous; she went into a coma and died an hour later.
Toklas was at her side before surgery when Stein asked, 'What is the
answer?' Toklas could not respond. 'Then what is the question?'

The American Hospital was opened in 1909–10 as a free hospital at
the corner of Boulevard du Château and rue Chauveau in Neuilly and
was surrounded by a park of six acres. The hospital no longer treats
Americans free of charge!

The church of Saint-Honoré-d'Eylau, in Place Victor-Hugo, where
Hemingway married Pauline Pfeiffer on 10 May 1927.

## 7  L'Eglise de Saint-Honoré-d'Eylau: 9 Place Victor-Hugo    16e

The church of Saint-Honoré-d'Eylau was the site of the marriage of

Hemingway and Pauline Pfeiffer on 10 May 1927, eleven days before Lindbergh made his solo flight to Paris. Virginia Pfeiffer was the witness for her sister; Hemingway wore a three-piece tweed suit, and Pauline wore a silk dress with a strand of pearls.

Over the centre door (entry on the left) is the scripture from Matthew 1:28 'Venez à moi . . . Come unto me, all ye that labour and are heavy laden'. The simple interior with the row of disciples across the back of the altar draws one's eyes to the larger circular stained-glass window above the altar.

The modest (for this neighbourhood) church is on the corner of Avenue Victor-Hugo and rue Mesnil, facing the fountain of three bowls in the centre of Place Victor-Hugo. Pauline's apartment, where she and Hemingway had been meeting during the year before, is two blocks away in elegant little rue Picot, up tree-lined Avenue Bugeaud.

The last Fitzgerald home is just three blocks away. Walk up rue Mesnil, beside the church, then left in front of the old market at the end of the street, and right into rue des Sablons. Note the old artists' studios at No. 11 on the left. At the next intersection (Place du Mexico), turn right into rue de Longchamp, which affords a framed view of the Eiffel Tower. A few steps ahead on your left is rue Herran, an exclusive little street that offers private parking slots only for its residents. The Fitzgerald residence is an elegant, high-ceilinged 1896 building.

## 8  F. Scott Fitzgerald: 4 rue Herran                    16e

The Fitzgeralds apparently lived here briefly, during May of 1930, around the corner from the Murphys' apartment.

He wrote to his agent, Harold Ober, that he was working on a short story, but that Zelda was 'seriously ill'. Soon her condition demanded immediate attention, and in June Scott took her to a sanatorium in Switzerland. She was diagnosed as schizophrenic and treated. Almost a year and a half later the Fitzgeralds left for the United States.

There is some evidence that the Fitzgeralds lived in rue des Marbonniers, south of here near Radio-France, sometime in 1930 before moving to rue Herran.

Continue down rue Herran to where it turns left. Walk straight toward the Murphy house at the end of this mansion-lined street. The Thai Embassy is at No. 8 and the Spanish Embassy is at No. 6.

## 9   Gerald and Sara Murphy: 2 rue Greuze                 16e

Wealthy American friends (and fellow *bons vivants*) of Scott and Zelda Fitzgerald, as well as of the Diaghilev ballet, the Murphys kept homes in Paris and on the Riveria during the decade they lived in France. Gerald studied painting with Fernand Léger and Sara entertained grandly. Hemingway, Fitzgerald, Dos Passos, and numerous other Americans were guests at their homes. Fitzgerald dedicated *Tender is the Night* to the Murphys, who were in part the inspiration for his Dick and Nicole Diver; and he took the name of their daughter Honoria for 'Babylon Revisited'. Thanks to the Murphys, the Fitzgeralds, whose rue de Tilsitt home was straight up Avenue Kléber, met all the 'right people' in Paris. The Murphys moved from a house on the Left Bank to this elegant new neighbourhood below the Arc de Triomphe, between the Bois de Boulogne and the Seine.

The Murphy home is on the corner of rue Greuze and Avenue Georges-Mandel. Across the avenue is the Passy cemetery, where Edouard Manet, Claude Debussy, and Jean Giraudoux are buried.

Turn left into Avenue Georges-Mandel and then right around the Place du Trocadéro, in front of the cemetery with its monument to the dead of the First World War. The two wings of the Chaillot Palace (1937) to your left contain museums: maritime and man, right; architecture, sculpture, and cinema, left. Walk toward the corner park and Avenue Franklin beside the museum.

## 10   Benjamin Franklin and Yorktown Square                 16e

The small park that forms the intersection of Avenue Franklin and rue Vineuse is dedicated to the Americans and the French who died helping the American colonies secure their freedom from the British. The next stop will commemorate the Americans who fought for French freedom on European soil. These two commemorative sites testify to the historical ties between France and the United States.

This lovely little park with the tall trees behind it honours Benjamin Franklin, the favourite American in Paris in the eighteenth century. At the tip of the park, in front of the large statue of the seated Franklin (boyhood model for Fitzgerald's Jay Gatsby), is a plaque placed there in 1983 at the bicentennial celebration of the Treaties of Paris and Versailles, signed by Franklin. As you round the park, you will see another monument, erected to commemorate the French who died at Yorktown in 1781 assisting

Benjamin Franklin, France's favourite American in the eighteenth
century, presides over Yorktown Square in the elegant 16th
arrondissement.

American independence — hence the name of the square.
As you walk down Avenue Franklin, you pass the top part of Chaillot

Gardens to your left. Franklin runs into Place de Costa-Rica and rue Raynouard begins directly opposite.

In the Place de Costa-Rica, look right for rue de la Tour, which begins here and runs to the Bois de Boulogne. Near the park lived a French critic and translator important to Fitzgerald, Hemingway, and other American moderns. Victor Llona was a friend of the authors and the translator of Fitzgerald's *The Great Gatsby* and 'The Baby Party', and Hemingway's 'Now I Lay Me' and 'The Killers'. He also translated Dreiser's *An American Tragedy* and works by Anderson, Cather, Dos Passos, Bromfield, and numerous British writers.

As you enter rue Raynouard, you will see No. 21 with the bay windows straight ahead of you.

## 11   Malcolm Cowley and the American Field Service: 21 rue Raynouard                                                        16e

Here you find the site of another one of the most important links between the United States and France: the headquarters of the American Field Service in France, a noncombat medical organization during the First World War. Malcolm Cowley and many other future writers served with the French military transport service (Hemingway had served with the Red Cross Ambulance Service) that worked out of this office. Joining Cowley from Harvard were Dos Passos, Cummings, and Robert Hillyer. From Columbia were Louis Bromfield and Slater Brown. Hemingway considered war a 'great experience' for a writer.

Beginning in May 1917, Cowley wrote long letters to Kenneth Burke (then a student at Harvard, later a critic for *The Dial*) in which he describes Paris: 'no militarists over here', 'the whores are thick in the rue du Montmartre'; the ambulance corps: 'I am the poorest driver in camp' according to 'conceited young puppies from Andover'; and his plans to write poetry and be a farmer. He thinks of 'living in a garret in Montmartre' and being French 'temporarily'. In a letter dated 31 July 1917 he expresses a common American attitude:

> I thank God constantly that I have crossed the water. Not that my soul has been transformed with wonder, but just that I have been drawn out of my fixed orbit. Now I have the desire to wander, and think of Russia and Spain, and American lumber camps and wheatfields. There are so many sides of life which no one can afford to miss. Paris is one.

Later he called it 'salvation by exile'. Following the war Cowley studied at the University of Montpellier on an American Field Service Fellowship. This gave him 'an excellent perspective on America, and under its influences my ideas seem to be clarifying slowly'. 'It frightens me to see how dependent on environment I am', he confided to Burke.

There is a plaque on the new (1933) building that commemorates the volunteers:

> through the house that formerly stood here passed 2,437 American volunteers who served under the French flag. Their ambulances carried more than 400,000 wounded 'poilus' to safety and 127 gave their lives so that France might live    1914–1917.

Because the buildings on the left look out over the Seine and the Left Bank, this street offers the walker occasional views down toward the river. Do not miss seeing the beautiful fountain and garden at No. 23 or, as you return toward the Passy station or the Chaillot Gardens, the tiles and garden at No. 15. If you want to continue further up the street, you can see Maison de Balzac at No. 47 and another plaque to Benjamin Franklin at the corner of rue Singer. At 62 rue Raynouard (in the pavilion of the former Hôtel de Valentinois Nos 64–70), Benjamin Franklin lived grandly for eight years (1777–1785), entertaining every important visitor from America.

All trace of the next site has disappeared.

## 12  Vélodrome d'Hiver: 8 Boulevard de Grenelle     15e

Across the river from Passy métro (near the métro stop Bir-Hakeim and at the corner of rue Nelaton) was the site of the indoor stadium called 'Vél d'hiv', built in 1910. The Germans used it to round up Jews during the Second World War. It was torn down in 1959.

The stadium was popular with Hemingway in the 1920s. He came to watch boxing matches and the six-day bicycle races, dragging along many friends such as Sylvia Beach, Adrienne Monnier, and John Dos Passos. He always took his friends for, as Dos Passos noted, 'he had an evangelical streak that made him work to convert his friends to whatever mania he was encouraging at the time'. Most confessed later that they could not resist Hemingway but did not enjoy their experience. 'Most people seemed very vague beside him', explained Beach. He later told Hotchner he wrote the

40th draft of the end of *A Farewell to Arms* in a box at the finish line.

Toward the end of his life, Hemingway said

[I] started many stories about bicycle racing but have never written one that is as good as the races are . . . But I will get the Vélodrome d'Hiver with the smoking light of the afternoon and the high-banked wooden track and the whirring sound the tires made on the wood as the riders passed, the effort and the tactics as the riders climbed and plunged, each one a part of his machine.

He always wanted to capture the best experiences of his Paris years in his writing.

Hemingway did capture the streets, river banks, and cafés of Paris, infusing them with what, in an early feature piece he had written for the *Toronto Star*, he called 'magic': 'There is a magic in the name France. It is a magic like the smell of the sea or the sight of blue hills or of soldiers marching by. It is a very old magic.'

# SOURCES

Anderson, Margaret, *My Thirty Years' War: An Autobiography* (New York: Covici, Friede, 1930).

Asselineau, Roger, 'Hemingway in Paris', *Fitzgerald/Hemingway Annual 1973*, 11-32.

——,(ed.), *The Literary Reputation of Hemingway in Europe* (New York: New York University Press, 1965).

Baker, Carlos, *Ernest Hemingway: A Life Story* (New York: Scribner's, 1969).

——,*Hemingway: The Writer as Artist* (Princeton, NJ: Princeton University Press, 1956, 1972).

Bald, Wambly, *On the Left Bank 1929-1933*, ed. Benjamin Franklin, V. (Athens, Ohio: Ohio University Press, 1987).

Beach, Sylvia, *Shakespeare and Company* (New York: Harcourt Brace, 1959).

Beauvoir, Simone de, *Force of Circumstance*, trans. Richard Howard (Harmondsworth: Penguin, 1968).

Blackmur, R. P., 'The American Literary Expatriate', in *Foreign Influences in American Life*, ed. David F. Bowers (Princeton: Princeton University Press, 1944), 126-45.

Brian, Denis, *The Faces of Hemingway: Intimate Portraits of Ernest Hemingway by Those Who Knew Him* (London: Grafton Books, 1988).

Broyard, Anatole, 'About Books', *The New York Times Book Review* (15 December 1985), 10.

Bruccoli, Matthew J., *Scott and Ernest: The Authority of Failure and the Authority of Success* (New York: Random House, 1978).

Buckley, Peter, *Ernest* (New York: Dial, 1978).

Callaghan, Morley, *That Summer in Paris* (New York: Coward-McCann, 1963).

Calmer, Edgar, *All the Summer Days* (Boston: Little Brown, 1961).

Chamson, André, *La Petite Odyssée* (Paris: Gallimard, 1965).

Charters, James, *This Must Be the Place: Memoirs of Montparnasse* (London: Herbert Joseph, 1934).

Cowley, Malcolm, 'A Brief History of Bohemia', *Freeman* (19 July 1922), 439.

——, *Exile's Return: A Literary Saga of the 1920s* (New York: Viking, 1951).

——, *Second Flowering: Works and Days of the Lost Generation* (New York: Viking, 1973).

——, 'This Youngest Generation', *New York Evening Post Literary Review* (15 October 1921), 81-2.

Cummings, E. E., *The Enormous Room* (New York: Random House, 1949 (1922)).

——, *i: Six Nonlectures* (Cambridge: Harvard University Press, 1953).

——, *Is 5* (New York: Liveright, 1926).

Dos Passos, John. *The Best Times: An Informal Memoir* (New York: New American Library, 1966).

——, *The Fourteenth Chronicle: Letters & Diaries*, ed. Townsend Ludington (Boston: Gambit, 1973).

Ellmann, Richard, *James Joyce* (New York: Oxford University Press, 1982).

Faulkner, William, *Sanctuary* (New York: Modern Library, Random House, 1921, 1958).

——, *Selected Letters*, ed. Joseph Blotner (New York: Random House, 1977).

Felton, Charles A., *The Apprenticeship of Ernest Hemingway* (New York: Viking, 1954).

Fitch, Noël Riley, *Literary Cafés of Paris* (Washington DC: Starrhill Press, 1989).

——, *Sylvia Beach and the Lost Generation: A History of Literary Paris in the Twenties and Thirties* (New York: Norton, 1983; Harmondsworth: Penguin, 1985).

Fitzgerald, F. Scott, *The Crack Up*, ed. Edmund Wilson (New York: New Directions, 1945).

——, 'How to Live on Practically Nothing A Year', *The Saturday Evening Post* (20 September 1924) 17, 165-6, 169-70.

——, 'This Youngest Generation', *New York Evening Post Literary Review* (15 October 1921), 81-2.

——, *Tender is the Night* (New York: Scribner's, 1934).

——, *Letters of F. Scott Fitzgerald*, ed. Andrew Turnbull (New York: Scribner's, 1963).

——, *Stories of F. Scott Fitzgerald*, ed. Malcolm Cowley. (New York: Scribner's, 1951).

'Fitzgerald and Hemingway in Paris: Conference Proceedings,' *Fitzgerald/Hemingway Annual 1973*.

Flanner, Janet, *Paris Was Yesterday 1925-1939*, ed. Irving Drutman (New York: Viking, 1972).

Ford, Ford Madox, *It Was the Nightingale* (New York: Octagon, 1975 (1934)).

Ford, Hugh (ed.), *The Left Bank Revisited: Selections from the Paris Tribune, 1917-1934* (University Park: Penn State University Press, 1972).

Gajdusek, Robert E., *Hemingway and Joyce: A Study in Debt and Payment* (Corte Madre, CA: Square Circle, 1984).

——, *Hemingway's Paris* (New York: Scribner's, 1978).

Le Gallienne, Richard, *From a Paris Garret* (New York: Ives Washburn, 1936).

Gilot, Françoise and Charlton Lake, *Life with Picasso* (New York: New American Library, 1965).

Glassco, John, *Memoirs of Montparnasse* (Toronto: Oxford University Press, 1970).

Hawkins, Eric, *Hawkins of the Paris Herald* (New York: Simon & Schuster, 1963).

Hemingway, Ernest, *By-Line: Ernest Hemingway*, ed. William White. (New York: Scribner's, 1968).

——, *Green Hills of Africa* (New York: Scribner's, 1935, 1963).

——, *The Nick Adams Stories* (New York: Scribner's, 1972).

——, *Islands in the Stream* (New York: Scribner's, 1970).

——, *A Moveable Feast* (New York: Scribner's, 1964).

——, *Selected Letters*, ed. Carlos Baker (New York: Scribner's, 1981).

——, 'The Snows of Kilimanjaro', in *The Short Stories of Ernest Hemingway* (New York: Scribner's, 1938, 1966).

——, *The Sun Also Rises* (New York: Scribner's, 1926, 1954).

——, 'Wild Night Music of Paris Makes Visitor Feel a Man of the World.' *The Star Weekly*, Toronto (25 March 1922).

Hemingway, Jack, *Misadventures of a Fly Fisherman: My Life With and Without Papa* (New York: McGraw-Hill, 1986).

Hemingway, Mary Welsh, *How It Was* (New York: Knopf, 1976).

Hillairet, Jacques, *Dictionnaire historique des rues de Paris* (Paris: Editions de Minuit, 1961).

Hoffman, Frederick J., *The Twenties: American Writing in the Postwar Decade* (New York: Macmillan, 1962).

Hotchner, A. E., *Papa Hemingway* (New York: Random House, 1966).

Huddleston, Sisley, *Back to Montparnasse* (Philadelphia: J. B. Lippincott, 1931).

——, *Paris Salons, Cafés, Studios: Being Social, Artistic and Literary Memories* (Philadelphia: J. B. Lippincott, 1928).

Hulme, Kathryn C., *Undiscovered Country: A Spiritual Adventure* (Boston: Little Brown, 1966).

James, Henry, *The Ambassadors* (New York: W. W. Norton, 1964).

Joost, Nicholas, *Ernest Hemingway and the Little Magazines: The Paris Years* (Barre, MA: Barre Publishers, 1968).

Josephson, Matthew, *Life Among the Surrealists* (New York: Holt, Rinehart & Winston, 1962).

Kert, Bernice, *The Hemingway Women* (New York: W. W. Norton, 1983).

Knoll, Robert, E. (ed.), *McAlmon and the Lost Generation* (Lincoln: University of Nebraska Press, 1957).

Kohner, Frederick, *Kiki of Montparnasse* (London: Cassell, 1968).

Laney, Al, *Paris Herald: The Incredible Newspaper* (New York: Appleton-Century, 1947).

Le Gallienne, Richard, *From a Paris Garret* (New York: Washburn, 1936).

Lewis, Sinclair, *Dodsworth* (New York: Harcourt Brace, 1929).

——, 'Self-Conscious America', *The American Mercury* (October 1925), 129-39.

Llona, Victor, 'I Knew Them in Paris: A Translator recalls the Years Between the Wars', ed. Ernest Kroll (Unpublished memoirs).

Loeb, Harold, *The Professors Like Vodka* (Carbondale: Southern Illinois University Press, 1974 (1927)).

——, *The Way It Was* (New York: Criterion Books, 1959).

Lynn, Kenneth, *Hemingway* (New York: Simon & Schuster, 1987).

Ludington, Townsend, *John Dos Passos: A 20th Century Odyssey* (New York: E. P. Dutton, 1980).

MacLeish, Archibald, *A Continuing Journey: Essays and Addresses* (Boston: Houghton Mifflin, 1968).

——, *New and Collected Poems* (Boston: Houghton Mifflin, 1985).

——, 'There Was Something About the Twenties', *Saturday Review* (31 December 1966), 10-13.

——, 'What one remembers . . . ', *Mercure de France*, Memorial Edition to Sylvia Beach, No. 349 (August/September, 1963), 34-5.

Marquez, Gabriel García, 'Gabriel García Marquez meets Ernest Hemingway', *The New York Times Book Review* (26 July 1984), 1, 16-17.

Maurice, Arthur Bartlett, *The Paris of the Novelists* (Garden City, NY: Doubleday Page, 1919).

Mayfield, Sarah, *Exiles from Paradise: Zelda and Scott Fitzgerald* (New York: Delacorte, 1971).

Mellow, James R., *Charmed Circle: Gertrude Stein & Company* (New York: Avon, 1975).

——, *Invented Lives: F. Scott and Zelda Fitzgerald* (Boston: Houghton Mifflin, 1984).

Meral, Jean, *Paris dans la littérature américaine* (Paris: Editions du CNRS, 1983).

Milford, Nancy, *Zelda* (New York: Harper & Row, 1970).

Miller, Henry, *The Tropic of Cancer* (New York: Grove, 1961).

McAlmon, Robert, *Being Geniuses Together 1920-1930*, revised with Kay Boyle (New York: Doubleday, 1968).

Monnier, Adrienne, *The Very Rich Hours of Adrienne Monnier,* trans. Richard McDougall (New York: Scribner's, 1976).

Morton, Brian, *Americans in Paris* (Ann Arbor: Olivia & Hill, 1984).

Motherwell, Hiram, 'The American Tourist Makes History', *Harpers Magazine* (December 1929), 70-6.

Mowrer, Paul Scott, *The House of Europe* (Boston: Houghton Mifflin, 1945).

Nin, Anaïs. *Paris Revisited* (Santa Barbara: Capra, 1972).

Orwell, George, *Down and Out in Paris and London* (San Diego: Harcourt Brace Jovanovich, 1961 (1933)).

Paul, Elliot, *The Last Time I Saw Paris* (New York: Random House, 1942).

Plimpton, George, 'Ernest Hemingway: An Interview', *The Paris Review* (Spring 1958), 61-89.

Poli, Bernard J., *Ford Madox Ford and the Transatlantic Review* (Syracuse, NY: Syracuse University Press, 1967).

Porter, Katherine Anne, 'A Little Incident in the Rue de l'Odéon', *Ladies Home Journal,* Vol. 81 (August 1964), 54-5.

Pound, Ezra, *Make it New: Essays by Ezra Pound* (New Haven: Yale University Press, 1939).

——, *Personae: The Collected Poems of Ezra Pound.* (New York: New Directions, 1954).

Putnam, Samuel, *Paris Was Our Mistress: Memoirs of a Lost and Found Generation* (Carbondale: Southern Illinois University Press, 1970 (1947)).

Reynolds, Michael S., *The Young Hemingway: A Literary Biography* (New York: Oxford University Press, 1986).

Robertson, Charles L., *The International Herald Tribune* (New York: Columbia University Press, 1987).

Rood, Karen Lane (ed.), *American Writers in Paris 1920-1939, Dictionary of Literary Biography,* Vol. 4 (Detroit: Gale Research, 1980).

Sarason, Bertram D. (ed.), *Hemingway and 'The Sun' Set* (Washington, DC: Microcard Editions, 1972).

Seldes, George, *Witness to a Century: Encounters with the Noted, the Notorious, and the Three SOBs* (New York: Ballantine, 1987).

Shirer, William, *20th Century Journey: A Memoir of a Life and the Times: The Start 1904-1930* (New York: Simon & Schuster, 1976).

Singer, Bruce (ed.), *A Century of News: From the Archives of the International Herald Tribune* (1988).

Sokoloff, Alice Hunt, *Hadley: The First Mrs Hemingway* (New York: Dodd, Mead, 1973).

Solano, Solita, 'Paris Between the Wars: An Unpublished Memoir', ed. John C. Broderick. *Quarterly Journal of the Library of Congress,* Vol. 34. No. 4 (October 1977), 306-14.

Stearns, Harold, *Confessions of a Harvard Man: Paris and New York in the 1920s and 1930s* (West Sutton: Paget Press, 1984). (Originally *The Street I Know,* 1935).

Stein, Gertrude, *Paris France* (New York: Liveright, 1970).

——, *The Autobiography of Alice B. Toklas* (New York: Random House, 1933, 1960).

Stephens, Robert O., *Hemingway's Non-Fiction: The Public Voice.* (Chapel Hill: University of North Carolina, 1968).

Stock, Noel, *The Life of Ezra Pound* (New York: Random House, 1970).

Stoneback, H. R. 'From the rue Saint-Jacques to the Pass of Roland to the unfinished Church on the Edge of the Cliff', *The Hemingway Review,* Vol. 1, No. 1 (Fall 1986), 2-20.

Tate, Allen, *Memoirs and Opinions 1926-1974* (Chicago: Swallow, 1975).

Tavernier-Courbin, Jacqueline, 'The Paris Notebooks', *The Hemingway Review*, Vol. 1, No. 1 (Fall 1981), 23-6.

Toklas, Alice B., *What is Remembered* (San Francisco: North Point Press, 1985).

Tomkins, Calvin, *Living Well is the Best Revenge* (New York: Viking, 1971).

Le Vot, André, *F. Scott Fitzgerald: A Biography* (Garden City: Doubleday, 1983).

Weld, John, *Young Man in Paris* (Chicago: Academy, 1985).

Wescott, Glenway, 'A Sentimental Contribution', *Hound and Horn* (April–June 1934), 523-34.

West, Nathanael, *The Dream Life of Balso Snell* (Paris: Contact, 1931).

Wickes, George, *The Amazon of Letters: The Life and Loves of Natalie Barney* (New York: G. P. Putnam, 1976).

——, *Americans in Paris* (Garden City: Doubleday, 1969).

Williams, William Carlos. *Autobiography* (New York: New Directions, 1967 (1951)).

Wiser, William, *The Crazy Years* (New York: Atheneum, 1983).

Wolfe, Thomas, *Of Time and the River* (New York: Scribner's, 1935).

——, *The Web and the Rock* (New York: Scribner's, 1939).

Wolff, Geoffrey, *Black Sun: The Brief and Violent Eclipse of Harry Crosby* (New York: Random House, 1976).

# INDEX